TEACHING EARLY ADOLESCENTS CREATIVELY:
A Manual for Church School Teachers

by EDWARD D. SEELY

w

THE WESTMINSTER PRESS
Philadelphia

ISBN 0-664-24927-2
LIBRARY OF CONGRESS CATALOG CARD NO. 71-155903

1. Youth - Education.

I . Title.

PUBLISHED BY THE WESTMINSTER PRESS ®
PHILADELPHIA, PENNSYLVANIA

PRINTED IN THE UNITED STATES OF AMERICA

Contents

Preface

"THANK YOU VERY MUCH for asking, Pastor, but I'm in so many things now that I just won't have the time to do the job justice." With that explanation, Mr. Smith joined a growing list of people who with varying but extraordinarily similar responses have been trying as politicly as possible to excuse themselves from teaching a junior high Sunday school class for the coming year.

Upon first looking at the situation, the frustrated recruitment officer of the Sunday school, or the pastor, or whoever has been given the responsibility of procuring teachers for the junior high department begins to feel that those who have declined his offer are afraid of these young people. He believes they feel inadequate and don't want to teach because they really don't know how. He is partly right.

However, another factor is involved. Where does a person find resources to aid him in his attempt to provide for the Christian nurture of youth in their early adolescence? Psychologists and educators have only recently come to see the early teen-ager as a quite different person who faces quite different situations and has quite different needs from the later teen-ager.

Moreover, behavioral scientists are also finding it necessary to group eleven- and twelve-year-olds with early teens, an approach increasingly utilized in secular education's movement to the middle school concept, for the future of the Christian education of this age group. Hence, resources written especially to help one who aspires to relate to junior high young people within the context of Christian education are very limited. Yet, many fine secular works are being produced today, a number of which will be referred to in the following pages, that bring to light physiological, sociological, and psychological principles extremely well suited to the Christian education situation and beneficial for the Christian growth of the junior high youth.

The problem now becomes, How can a transfer be effected whereby a church school teacher can utilize these principles to further the Christian nurture of the young people under his tutelage? So stated, that is the purpose of this book. Using the best principles in the above three fields which lend themselves to educational methodology, combined with this author's personal experience in utilizing them through writing curricula and in teaching junior highs, it will be the general goal of this work to provide the teacher with a handbook of practical classroom resources that are also Biblically and theologically sound.

Certain grateful acknowledgments must be made to people without whose encouragement and talents this work could not have become a reality. They are many, but I am especially grateful to The Reverend Hugh Koops, Assistant Professor of Christian Ethics at New Brunswick Theological Seminary, for his strengthening counsel and friendship; Dr. Dennis Hoekstra, Assistant Dean for Academic Affairs of Calvin College, who took much time from his busy schedule to read the manuscript and make helpful suggestions for its improvement; Mrs. Franklin Rynbrandt, faithful and dedicated secretary of the Fifth Reformed Church, Grand Rapids, who accomplished the laborious task of typing; and my family, especially my wife, Carol, and daughter, Jan, for their love, understanding, and patience during the absence of their husband and father from their fellowship.

E. D. S.

Introduction

BEFORE WE BEGIN, we need to look briefly at four assumptions that will provide the basis and meaning for the discussion to follow. These assumptions are: (1) that the Holy Spirit is the chief agent of Christian nurture and that our purpose is mainly to provide the context in which he can work; (2) that the whole Bible, the Old and the New Testament, is used as the basic point of reference and ultimate source of truth in the class, with emphasis on those passages which portray Jesus Christ as Lord and Savior; (3) that what a teacher communicates nonverbally is as important and teaches as much as what he says with words; and (4) that a fully committed teacher (i.e., one who identifies himself as a Christian) is more important than any materials.

In regard to the first assumption, few if any of the people who have taught for any length of time in Christian education would deny that at times they felt frustrated and thought their work was futile. Throughout history this has been the experience which man has had, especially when he has relied too much upon himself and not enough upon God for his help. Human beings are limited; God is unlimited. We are finite; he is infinite. We must not expect too much of ourselves. By ourselves, we can accomplish little in the tremendously great task of Christian education, yet we too will find with the apostle Paul that we can do all things through relying on the Lord for our help (Phil. 4:13).

The second assumption, that the Bible is the basic resource book in the class, means that the Bible is seen to be the ultimate authority with regard to questions which the class encounters. We must use it as an instrument through which our students can hear God speak to their lives. "Basic resource" also means that we should teach the Bible, especially those passages of the New Testament which present Jesus Christ as our only Lord and Savior, and the implications of this fact for the life situations of our junior highs.

Hence, when the two goals of Christian education, which will be discussed in a number of contexts, are referred to as the attempt to develop the ability to share our faith and to develop the sensitivity and ability to meet human needs, the basic assumption behind the first goal is that our students are dealing with the root facts upon which they can build a faith to share. At the junior high age the stress should be on applying the facts of faith to the working out of the student's responsibility under the Great Commission.

Most witnessing, if a student is effectively sharing his faith, will be accomplished away from the church. However, if non-Christian youth are brought to the church school class, they will receive the gospel message through communication with the friend with whom they came and in the Bible study mentioned above. Also, as we will see in conjunction with the description of adolescent identity, there is opportunity to help each student identify with Christ as a means of fulfilling his identity. But the emphasis will be on what all this means in terms of application to his daily life situation.

The third assumption which occurs throughout this study is that what you as a teacher do is as important as what you say. Students acquire values communicated by the teacher through both word and deed. You can undo with your actions what you speak with words. If, for example, you say you believe that the Bible is important but never use it in class or live its principles, there is no way to make your pupils believe you or place a high value on the Bible for themselves. That is why Paul admonished Titus, who would be teaching, to be a model of what he taught (Titus 2:7). He undoubtedly was basing his caution upon the concept wrapped up in the ancient Hebrew word *dabar,* which means both "word" and "deed" at the same time. The two go hand in hand.

Yet, while there is an inherent danger in the communication that is nonverbal, there is also great power that can be put to use in Christian education. Such a use is ancient. God has employed nonverbal communication from time immemorial (Ps. 8:3–4; 19:1–6), and it is of sufficient value to render unrepenting and unbelieving men without excuse (Rom. 1:18 to 2:29). The many implications for learning by nonverbal communication will be discussed at different points throughout the remainder of our study.

Finally, the fourth assumption is that the committed Christian teacher, who is such through the love of Jesus Christ as his Savior and Lord and who places him above all else, is more important in the learning process than any material resources. This book can only hope to supplement the work of a dedicated teacher, offering him means through which he can improve his classroom communication. It cannot, however, make a good teacher out of a person who doesn't love Christ and want to transmit that love and to dedicate himself to the Lord's service.

A textbook should be seen as only a guide to making Biblical truth clear and as the barest minimum of input for class learning. As the teacher reads the text, he should do so in the light of the question, How can I make it possible for the student to discover the truth of each point and relate it to his life's needs? In order to answer that question the teacher will have to know what those needs are, how learning that results in transfer to behavior takes place, and which methods will stimulate that learning. We will now consider those topics in that order.

PART I

FOUNDATION
FOR BUILDING

1

Physiological Development

SUDDENLY THE STABLE, certain, secure world of the new adolescent seems terribly chaotic. It is no longer logical—as he knew logic. He just can't understand it. Sometimes he simply doesn't know where he stands: it seems as though he were in two different worlds, and, in a very real sense, he is.

The youth's first awareness of this tremendous change starts to dawn upon him when he begins to see certain notable differences in his own physical makeup. Upon further examination he finds himself to be an entirely dissimilar person from the individual who walked in his tennis shoes only a few weeks ago; he is an entirely different person biologically. He does not have a child's body; he has an adult's body, or at least the beginnings of one. He doesn't look the same, sound the same, or feel the same. He has entered the stage of puberty, and in so doing he has also crossed the threshold of adolescence.

Puberty is not coterminous with but is the beginning of adolescence from a physiological point of view. Puberty, from the Latin *pubes,* meaning "adult" or "of ripe age," refers to the maturation of human sexuality, specifically the ability to procreate.

There is much fuzziness in the way our American culture treats this subject, and this obscurity undoubtedly has no little effect upon the identity struggle which junior high young people experience. Physiologically, adolescence can begin as early as nine or ten for girls, though the exceptions to the thirteen-year median age are usually within the eleven to twelve range for both girls and boys who become physically mature early. Sociologically, however, our society considers a young person an adolescent when he becomes thirteen ("adolescent" and "teen-ager" being synonymous in the minds of American people). One can see how confusing this would be to an early (or late) bloomer. However, more salt is added to the wound. Psychological integration of all the forces the new adolescent feels within himself does not come until much later. With cultural confusion added, the period of personal conflict is extended even beyond what it should be. This all boils down to the realization of what will be a common strand running through the entire length of this book: each junior high youth is a unique individual and he will have to be related to as an entity unto himself unlike all others in very important ways before he can be understood and known as a person. This understanding and knowing is the first and most integral dimension of his Christian nurture.

For a time before the beginning of puberty, the anterior lobe of the pituitary gland, a small pea-size organ located at the base of the brain, emits secretions that stimulate the growth and activity of the gonads, the ovaries of the female and the testes of the male. The gonads also begin to produce estrogen (a female sex hormone) and androgen (a male sex hormone). These changes in the adolescent's body are referred to as primary sex characteristics; they give rise to secondary sexual changes.

In girls such secondary alterations include a widening and rounding of the hips, the appearance of pubic hair on the lower abdomen, the beginning of menstruation, the development of the breasts, and the leveling off of the growth rate, the period of the most rapid growth in height being about two years prior to menstruation. Such developments often create problems for the young lady, because they do not take place in an even manner. For example, well-documented medical studies demonstrate that while boys and girls have almost the same amount of fat at age twelve, two years later the former have reduced their amount of fat and increased in muscle while the latter have accomplished just the opposite. Moreover, the increasingly figure-conscious girl usually doesn't have an even distribution of her fat until the middle or later teens.

In boys the onset of puberty is less conspicuous, since there is no readily evident occurrence such as the beginning of menstruation to mark the event. A number of measures have been offered as points of reference; one, the appearance of pubic hair on the lower abdomen, has been used by Kinsey, who concluded in a 1948 study that the average age of the beginning of puberty in boys in the United States was between 13.7 and 14.6.

Other secondary characteristics of the physical development of the adolescent boy are an increase in the size of his penis and testes, growth of hair under the arms then on the face, widening of the shoulders and growth in height. Many boys now have caught up to the girls in height, and by the last year of junior high will be taller. At about that time, the voice will deepen in pitch.

As these physical changes occur without order and not all at the same time, the junior high is presented with one of his greatest problems. Since he can best describe it, let us listen as he explains his situation to a person well-known for her empathy:

> Dear Ann Landers: I am a 14-year-old boy who acts dumb and feels like everybody is looking at him and thinking "What a knothead!" I say dumb things to get attention and when I get the attention I am embarrassed and wish they would look at somebody else. As you can see, I'm a nut. I feel awkward and ugly and my face has the beginning of acne and my hands and feet are too big for the rest of me. Please tell me what it takes to get over these faults.
>
> —Mr. Nothing [1]

What was Ann's answer? "About four years—maybe less. But be patient, pal, you're more normal than you think." [2]

With the maturing of the physical dimensions of the human body comes another force that adds fuel to the fire that is providing the heat of the new adolescent's anxieties: the upsurge of the sex drive. The youth, very much aware of this development experiences new and exciting sensations which create a euphoria hitherto unimagined, and during which he or she is free from many other cares that trouble and concern.

Thus, according to the medical profession, many young people in this age group engage in masturbation. They do this as a result of experimentation with the new power they have found within themselves, and as a desire to escape from reality occasionally, even if for only a very short period of time. This activity is reported to be especially common in boys and is also frequently engaged in by girls.

Implications

What do all these physical changes mean for you, their teacher? Let us look at some specific implications for your role:

1. *Accept each student as he is.*

Your acceptance of each junior high young person, just as he is, unconditionally (this is not to be confused with condoning all his behavior; rather, it means the approval of him as a person who was created and is loved by God), will be teaching without the use of words a vital part of the gospel message and will be providing the context in which the best Christian education can occur. Ever since he was a child the adolescent has had the human need to be noticed and accepted; this need first appeared in his relations with his parents, it followed him as he began to branch out into the larger world, and it continues with him now as he finds himself in relationship with adults outside his home. In these relationships the youngster finds that he must have an emotional reference point, and adults who exercise authority over him take on the role formerly filled almost exclusively by his parents; hence it is to these new powers that he turns for rewards. An adult authority figure such as a teacher often becomes a substitute parent in his mind, especially if he feels close to the teacher. Most youth desire the acceptance and affection of these parent substitutes, even though their actions may seem to indicate just the opposite.

2. *Accent the positive.*

In addition to your own acceptance of the struggling adolescent, you can help create a climate of acceptance in the class setting. By "failing to notice" when John trips over a desk when he enters the room instead of castigating him for being clumsy, and by refraining from comments such as, "You're getting a little heavy, aren't you, Sally?" Or, more positively, you can develop an atmosphere of acceptance through stressing or at least pointing out the good things your students do, the points they make in a discussion which are helpful and informative, and facts about them such as: "Say, Dave, nice going on getting First Class at the Scout Court of Honor last Wednesday! I saw your picture in the paper."

3. *Treat them as young people growing into adulthood.*
Since they are desirous of being accepted for what they are, adolescents, don't talk down to them or speak to them as though they were still children. Junior high young people are very sensitive about their age and feel quite hurt when they are treated as children. In other cultures special rites and ceremonies publicly proclaim the identity of the youth. Even within our own culture, Jewish people, celebrating the ancient *Bar Mitzvah* ceremony attempt to accomplish this recognition for their male young people. After the thirteen-year-old Jewish boy receives his cap and shawl, he is formally addressed from then on as "Mr." The only problem he encounters is when he leaves the synagogue and confronts the world outside which is unbelievably insensitive to his needs. However, you, the teacher of young people in this age range, can provide this function of the *Bar Mitzvah* through relating to each individual junior high as he is and not as if he were a child. In fact, you may well be able to go even farther, since the youth will realize that there is no rule requiring you to treat him in this manner.

4. *Examine your own feelings concerning sex.*

Since sex is such an important factor in the life of each of your students, and since masturbation can be a result of such preoccupation, carefully examine your own feelings on such matters, for your own emotional framework will be providing the motivation for all you do and say pertaining to these subjects. Approach your students not with a judgmental attitude when they show an interest in such topics but with love and understanding. Do not discourage their consideration of these subjects, for dealing with them in the light of Christian teaching will help you to minister greatly to their human needs at these points and will not force them to go to less desirable sources for their sex "education." Where you do sense an overstressing of sex, help them focus, either individually or as a group if a number are struggling with this difficulty, on more creative and fulfilling activities.[3]

5. *Be sensitive to the effects of physical changes in their bodies.*

Keep these physical changes clearly in your mind as you relate to junior high young people, and allow your awareness of these changes to sensitize you to the difficulties they present to the youth; let this awareness govern your approach as you deal with your adolescents. For instance, if one of your girls comes to a meeting somewhat moody, do not upbraid her for not taking an active part; consider the physical effect of a menstrual period upon a woman and the additional conflicting feelings this occurrence has upon a girl who is just beginning to experience this dimension of womanhood as she struggles to integrate all that is happening to her into a growing self-concept and an appreciation of her developing identity. Rather, quietly understand and take care not to cut yourself off from her; be available, a constant caring source of love and acceptance to which she can turn for help if she feels the need. When she doesn't take an active part in some meeting, fine. Accept that. Simply let her feel your gladness that she is present and begin to draw out others to provide the bulk of the discussion.

2
Sociological Development

JUNIOR HIGH YOUNG PEOPLE are influenced not only by their physical qualities but also by the environment in which they live. The interpersonal relationships in which the young people exist are powerful factors that affect their emerging identity. In our increasingly complex twentieth-century American culture, adolescents find themselves members of many groups, both voluntarily and involuntarily, and subject to the norms of those relationships.

It has been said that in our society it is quite likely there are more groups than there are individuals. A young person can belong to the Boy (or Girl) Scouts, the football team (or cheerleaders), the school newspaper, and any of a growing number of elective clubs that are being provided for youth today. As a member of these groups he or she is guided both by written and unwritten rules of play that influence the molding of his or her personality.

This effect is also present in groups of which the youth is an unwilling member. The color of his skin places him in an ethnic group containing many dynamic forces that exert their weight upon him. The church that his parents attend and to which they bring him has in turn several subgroups of which he becomes a member, such as youth fellowship, Sunday school, and in a number of denominations, a catechism class. He is also an American, a northerner or a southerner or an easterner or a westerner. He attends a certain school and is a member of the seventh grade, which may have either a strict or a very permissive teacher. He is a citizen of a certain state and a city or town in that state, both of which expect certain behavior to become ingrained within him as part of his personality. Hence, it is easy to see that the societal influence upon youth is considerable to say the very least.

Perhaps sociologist Margaret Mead has best phrased the question which faces us at this point: Are the difficulties a young person encounters "due to being adolescent or to being adolescent in America"? [4] After comparing the American way of life with the cultural conditions of a primitive society and the resultant effect upon the youth of each, she concludes that adolescence is not in itself a period of stress and strain; it is cultural conditioning which causes these conflicts. That relationship between society and personal problems is stated more directly by psychiatrist Erik Erikson, who has demonstrated that "there is no individual anxiety which does not reflect a latent concern common to the immediate and extended group." [5]

Although the biological elements that we have already examined (and seen to constitute a very real cause of many of the difficulties that early teens encounter) tend to nullify the universality of Mead's contention, it must be recognized that social influences do weigh heavily upon the junior high. This fact will be further verified as we seek to understand why.

There is within man a drive that makes him want to live in groups wherein he can enjoy the fellowship of other men. In this connection Aristotle's observation that man is a social animal and John Donne's more poetic affirmation that "no man is an island" indicate the reality of man's social consciousness throughout history.

From the time a child enters school and begins to grow in the ability to develop and experience satisfaction in interpersonal relationships, his life becomes increasingly influenced by persons outside the home, particularly his peers and certain adults with whom he comes into contact in his community, notably teachers. Psychologist Arthur Jersild cites a study in which approximately two thirds of a group of seven-year-olds named close personal acquaintances (relatives and friends) as their identity figures, but when they became fifteen years of age only 3 percent of the youth chose close personal acquaintances as their ideals.[6]

In addition to the experience of satisfaction that a young person acquires as his need for fellowship is met through interpersonal group relationships, he also obtains another very crucial benefit from his peers, namely, the help they provide him as he struggles to put together a self-concept. They act as a mirror, reflecting their view of him: if he is accepted, he comes to view himself as acceptable; if he is viewed as a good writer, he sees a whole range of possible vocations having to do with literary accomplishment open up for him; if he is given the nickname Smiley, he sees himself as being able to contribute something to mankind which is very important —an uplifting element of cheer during a difficult time. Or if his peers reflect a view of him that is uncomplimentary, for example, that he is of no use to them and they desire to avoid him, he will then incorporate this also into his self-concept and come to have a very weak ego, with little self-confidence, unless somewhere he finds another group of peers who have a different standard of values and needs who accept and want him.

These groups are the crucibles where the raw ego is refined and modified, where harsh reality strips away unreal veneer as often cruel peer observations "tell it like it is," both verbally and nonverbally. While the outer shell is stripped away from the view of the youth himself, so that he is allowed to see himself somewhat and to begin building an identity, the veneer is not always removed enough to allow others to see the real person beneath. Since identity development is a long process, some sort of guard is needed to protect what is being formed in the mind of the insecure youth.

Yet for both insecure and relatively stable adolescents, the group relationships they encounter help equip them for the roles they are soon to take on for the remainder of their lives. In youth groups the adolescent seeks a framework for the developing and solidifying of his self-concept, which he sees as his ticket into the adult world.

Another dimension of the sociological influences upon an adolescent is directly tied to the biological processes taking place within him. Although he may be interested only in football, spaceships, and other boys when he enters junior high, by the time he leaves he will be more concerned about developing a special relationship with a certain brunette who has been causing his heart to beat faster whenever she appeared for Sunday school class. A similar occurrence will take place in the girls in your classes, with the notable exception that their dolls are most likely to take second place to boys before football succumbs to girls in the boys' fancy. The sensitive teacher will be aware of the frustration this will cause from a girl's point of view as the signals she sends out are jammed by the electricity still engendered by football in its waning months as a boy's first love.

Aspects of the American culture in which you live are also important influences upon the youngsters you will teach. Even though you are not teaching in an urban environment, you are nevertheless confronting many of the dynamics of such a situation, and by 1980 you will quite likely be part of the 80 percent of the American population living in an urban area.[7] In your class it won't be uncommon to have as many as a dozen different schools represented, since youngsters may commute to your church from many different specialized localities in distant parts of the city.

Such localities, especially prominent in suburban sections, create problems in the area of communication and control. Parents see their suburban residential communities as only living places, but they are total communities for their children. This situation creates an increasing sense of community among the children, but a disintegrating sense of community among their parents. Because of this lack of community, communication, and communion among parents, there is an absence of norms to govern the activities of young people. When, for example, a son is told to be in at ten o'clock on a Friday night and he responds saying, "All the other kids can stay out until eleven thirty, why can't I?" the parent is virtually defenseless against his offspring's next accusation of being overly harsh, not to mention the charge of being out of step with the times. The parent simply has no way of knowing whether or not this is true of all the other kids. However, a growing number of localities within cities have responded to this difficulty by organizing Parents League chapters and developing community-backed codes dealing with such subjects as hours, dating, and driving, for the purpose of channeling young people's activities in the right direction.

This time problem is only one little practicality which the existence of pluralism brings to the church. It presents a much greater burden than raising the question of what time the class swimming party should end, for it is symptomatic of a deeper and more pervasive phenomenon especially related to the twentieth century and American culture, though by no means limited to us. Pluralism not only of group but also of thought will affect both what and how you teach.

Finally, as we consider the social influences that reach and act upon the junior high, it is important to focus upon factors pertaining to the sociological entity of the family. As we have noted above, the family is not the only influence affecting the adolescent. This, however, by no means indicates that the family is without any or even a lot of influence, especially where strong relationships have been founded in early life.

Such considerations do not mean, though, that the going will or even can be smooth for the adolescent or for his family. As he struggles to mold a self-concept, it is necessary in his thinking to put as much mileage between himself and childhood as possible. Hence, he feels he doesn't want to be associated with younger siblings in the age range that he has just passed through. In this way he will clearly be understood by both himself and others to be an adolescent and not—definitely not—a child. Therefore, while he eschews helping brothers and sisters in the six-to-eleven age range, he feels a certain maturity when he helps a preschool sibling who is not old enough to be confused with himself. For similar reasons, he is willing to associate with older brothers and sisters.

A sad fact reported by the United States Department of Health, Education, and Welfare, the National Center for Health Statistics, presents one remaining sociological element that affects a growing number of junior highs and demands consideration at least briefly. The divorce rate, which has since a peak in 1945 been subject to fluctuation, has been climbing steadily during the last decade.[8] Moreover, the statistics on divorce do not adequately indicate the number of unhappy families that provide a climate of hatred, bitterness, and rejection in which they live. Many parents, unknown to statistical records, are living in a state of divorce as far as mutual love, concern, and acceptance are concerned but have refused to make their estrangement official through a public record of divorce for a variety of reasons including: the effect on their children or on the husband's (or wife's) career, fear of public opinion. As a result, their children often experience an atmosphere of continuously intense enmity, malevolence, and obduracy, all of which serves to retard their Christian nurture.

Implications

How can you as their teacher deal with these sociological influences upon your junior high young people? Let's identify several specific ways.

1. *Develop a personal relationship with each of your students.*

Recognizing that social interaction and the thoughts of

others weigh heavily upon young adolescents, it will be to your advantage and their Christian growth if you make as great an effort as you can to develop a personal relationship with your class members and at the same time create the opportunity wherein they can grow in a constructive and creative relationship with one another. There are equally sound theological reasons for such an effort. By establishing a personal relationship with our young people, we will greatly aid them in coming to comprehend the personal relationship God has with them through Christ. Otherwise, all the "content" we teach is as nothing; it becomes empty and meaningless, with no frame of reference to which to relate. Moreover, it would be good to keep in mind the fact that your real "content" will not be the diligent adherence to a given textbook so much as the development of a student's relationship to Christ in the light of the Word of God and personal interaction within the fellowship of his classmates and an adult who cares. In such a context you will be teaching, nonverbally, a powerful and Biblically accurate lesson concerning the nature of the church—that it is not brick and mortar but flesh and blood, and that the people of God who compose the church have a vital ministry to each other, as well as to the world as a whole, as they are "mutually encouraged by each other's faith" (Rom. 1:12), and as they "bear one another's burdens, and so fulfil the law of Christ" (Gal. 6:2). In so doing, they will be experiencing the deepest fulfillment and satisfaction through meeting their interpersonal needs not only on the horizontal level but also on and in the light of the vertical plane.

How is this climate of Christian community realized in the class situation? One way is to have informal get-togethers on days other than when the class regularly meets. Such gatherings can take the form of beach parties, picnics, or camp-outs in good weather. During the winter or on inclement days your young people would enjoy Christian fellowship at a bowling alley, Y.M.C.A. swimming party, or roller skating to cite only a few examples. Hayrides are popular, and perhaps a farmer who gives hayrides also has a sleigh drawn by horses in the winter. During such outings, plan a time for games and refreshments. There is within the human breast a magnetism for others with whom one is supping. This truth was utilized by Jesus at the Last Supper which Christians have described as Holy Communion. Certainly something very close to that can be achieved with your youth group as you all sit on the floor around pop and potato chips. And it doesn't have to be any more elaborate than that.

Another way to create a climate of Christian community with your group of junior highs is to utilize the tremendously important principle of pupil participation in the learning process. Through carefully planned questions designed to draw out group discussion, help them to develop their ability to express themselves and what they believe. By so doing, you will be aiding them greatly in building self-confidence in their ability to share their faith, not only with each other but also in witnessing situations that will enable them to fulfill their responsibility under the Great Commission (Matt. 28:16–20). However, be prepared for, and even encourage, a resultant disagreement if you detect (as you undoubtedly will) the presence of opinions that differ from those which are being expressed. It is inconceivable that once opinions begin to be voiced there will be total agreement, an element that was neither present nor desired in Bible times

(Job, ch. 32; Jer. 15:17; Matt. 18:15–20; Acts 15:2, 36–41; Gal. 2:11). Once disagreement is offered, you have a tremendous opportunity to teach without the lecture method the Christian concept of community as you help your young people to distinguish between accepting a person as and for what he is, a fellow human brother or sister loved by God (and therefore lovable to us), even while not accepting all that he says or does. While you are helping them to understand this fundamental difference between accepting a person as he is, though not necessarily accepting some of his words or actions, you will also be encouraging your group to meet each other's individual need to construct a self-concept that is built around a feeling of worthiness, acceptance, and importance. What is more, it will have the most realistic and sound theological and Biblical basis in that it will be grounded in their love and acceptance by God, which will provide the Light in which they can accept one another.

2. *Treat all students equally.*

It is crucial that you bear in mind always the very important role you play as one of the most significant adults in the students' lives outside their families. It is imperative that you do what you are helping them to discover they should do—to accept one another in spite of differences. Along with this dimension of your relationship to your young people is another item to watch out for: don't play favorites. It is very easy to show favoritism, verbally as well as nonverbally (the latter is often the more difficult to guard against, for it is often subconsciously done), because every teacher feels a natural warmth toward the serious student who tries to do all he should, who speaks out in discussions, and who is not a discipline problem. Yet it is hurting not only him but the others in the class when he is showered with affection by a well-meaning but unsuspecting teacher who does not realize the rejection he is causing the favorite to receive and the rejection he is unwittingly displaying toward the other members of the class. Furthermore, experiencing such rejection, recalcitrant students will simply amplify their misbehavior either to attempt pathetically to gain more attention (conceived by the offended as acceptance) or in rebellion to act out their displeasure toward the teacher who is hurting them by his rejection.

Hence, it is important to relate in love and acceptance to all your students as you build a personal relationship with each one. How is this accomplished? First, get to know and use frequently each student's name. This is very important to them. If some have nicknames, use them with the individual's permission. However, be careful here. It is important to receive an individual's permission before calling him by a nickname. There is a good chance that he may *not* like his nickname, so simply ask, "John, do you prefer to be called Swish or should I stick with John?" Second, arrive at class early and talk with your students informally about topics that are of significance and interest to them. Also, plan to stay around for a while after class if one of your young people would like to talk to you about something—anything! Don't be the first one out the door after the bell rings. Be available. Third, on the outings play with them and talk with them.

Fourth, at the first meeting of the year, have all the members of your class list on one side of a 3″ x 5″ card *without signing their names* all the probems they have. Then have them list on the other side of the card all the complaints they have. Their anonymity is extremely important for the honesty and meaningfulness of this exercise. Therefore, stress a couple of times at the outset that they are not to sign their names. After about ten minutes (five minutes at the most for each part of this task), collect the cards and study them when you prepare for your lesson each week to see how you can relate part of what you are studying to the difficulties they are encountering in their life situations. As you talk with them individually in the way suggested above, try to get deeper than what the Detroit Tigers did in their last game or how you hope it doesn't rain for the next couple of hours anyway. Try to develop a sensitivity to their concerns and feelings.

After talking for a while in a relatively chitchat fashion which seems to be the typical opening gambit in most conversations, keeping the 3″ x 5″ cards in mind, ask a question such as, "Say, Sue, how are things in school?" "Oh, pretty good, I guess." Your next response would be helpful if you could give her a "door" to open if she wishes to develop her thinking and her feelings more, to share something with you without feeling forced to do so, in other words, to allow her to close the door if she wishes to at this time. Such a response could be "Just 'pretty good'?" or "But you're not sure." If she senses you care and are interested, she may quite likely confide in you some of what she is struggling with. But even if she simply says, "Yeah, ha, ha," and it is obvious that at this time at least she would not like to go farther, do not be discouraged. You are on your way to a meaningful ministry wherein you will be making a valuable contribution to the lives of your junior highs and to the Kingdom of God. At least Sue and others will know that you care and are interested, genuinely interested, in them, and you will have your opportunity to help. One very important element of such interpersonal relationships that should go without saying but which must always be remembered is never to break a confidence. When a young person shares something with you, *tell no one*.

A fifth way to further a personal relationship with your students is to invite them as a group to come to your home once or twice a year. A spring and fall party at your home is an excellent way to develop a friendly relationship with your young people. Finally, a sixth way is an activity one junior high teacher used so effectively that he still has his former students coming to see him to discuss matters of importance to them, even though they are now adults. He established a meaningful relationship with these people by taking them out one at a time to a restaurant for a hamburger and Coke at lunchtime on a Saturday. This offered him a good opportunity to talk privately to each about matters that were important to them and to establish a relationship with each that served as a framework within which to develop most effectively their Christian nurture, horizontally as well as vertically, on a level with their peers and with Christ.

3. *Be a model of what you want your students to be.*
Although you are an important person to them, you are an adult and not another young person. You must relate to them as such. They do not want you to identify with them, for this is to deprive them of a model to use as a guide in reaching the fulfillment of their own identity. They see themselves in the process of becoming, and they want their "significant adult" who has already "arrived" to form somewhat of a goal to work toward. Undoubtedly this is part of what Paul had in mind when he instructed

Titus to "show yourself in all respects a model of good deeds, and in your teaching show integrity, gravity, and sound speech that cannot be censured" (Titus 2:7–8). Young people don't really want you to use their clichés, and they have told this teacher many times that neither are they at all impressed by adults who try to dress as they do. What they do want is for their teacher or sponsor, their model, to be himself or herself with no artificial exterior, to try in love and acceptance to understand them and their needs, entering into their lives as closely as possible, but without compromising his own identity and integrity at the same time.

4. *Teach the moral and ethical dimension of the Christian response to God.*

As your youngsters are evolving from children to adults, biologically, and as they experience the transformation of their interpersonal relationships in order to adjust to this new identity, they will be experiencing a twofold need. It will be important for you to accept them where they are. It is offensive to a young man or woman to be considered as a child. You will be able to tell how you treat them by asking yourself whether, deep down, you tend to view them as children or young people becoming adults. Also, in addition to their need to be accepted as they are agewise, they have the need to deal with moral issues in the light of their faith. They have arrived at a period of "readiness" to consider their own morality in relationship to that of others. It has been shown that at this time in their lives, persons outside the home become more and more important in determining character traits such as honesty, loyalty, responsibility. These persons become models for adulation and emulation; they include historical figures and fictional heroes and heroines as well as famous living individuals such as sports personalities, movie stars, and charismatic government officials. Such facts you can utilize very effectively in your teaching situation. Because your students are influenced by the morality of others, deal with ethical situations, especially those of a sexual nature, a subject upon which they are beginning to focus ever more centrally, and bring out the various views on these situations, being sure to include the Biblical view and your own as well. It is good to teach by so doing that Jesus is Lord over our physical as well as our "spiritual" lives. Too often Jesus is left at church, conveniently miles away from the nearest lovers' lane.

Keep a file on famous persons who speak out about their Christian faith and how it relates to their lives. Be sure to include the large number of college and professional athletes who are members of the Fellowship of Christian Athletes and who willingly and openly witness to their faith and its influence in their lives as it helps them in many different situations. Such illustrations offered in class are very helpful to your students. In addition, such persons often travel from city to city speaking to Christian groups. By being aware of such coming events, you can either plan to attend with your class, or by cooperating with other churches have such a speaker address your group.

5. *Work closely with the families of your young people.*
It is the parents who have the primary responsibility for the Christian nurture of their children (Deut. 6:4–9; Ps. 78:1–8), and as teachers it is our function to supplement their ministry with resources that are unavailable

to them. Such resources include: peers and trained adults through whom the Spirit of God is speaking, plus the use of technological media in the form of audio-visual aids. It is important to maintain contact with parents to share with them what you are studying, what you are doing in class, and what your goals are so that they can work with you. However, you must be careful *never* to divulge any confidences that have been extended to you by the children of these parents! Such communication also helps to motivate parents to encourage their children to attend church school.

6. *Be sensitive to the concerns of young people whose parents are divorced or separated.*

Your role as parent substitute will take on extra meaning for such youth. You can minister to them through things you say in certain lessons. This will also have bearing on how you teach them that God is their Father. You will quite likely want to explain how he is the perfection of Fatherhood in contrast to the way all earthly fathers and mothers fail at times and in certain relationships. You must be careful not to identify homes that are still physically intact as necessarily happy homes. This writer counseled with three junior high girls who came to him late one evening. One girl's parents were divorced, and she was happier and more emotionally well-adjusted than were the other two who lived in homes of hatred. The fact that a child comes from a broken home does not mean that he or she will be delinquent, neurotic, or emotionally damaged. But such young people have many deep needs which have been created by such a situation, and you as their teacher can in most cases provide a valuable resource for dealing with those needs.

7. *Emphasize the Christian absolute.*

A seventh dimension of the sociological development of our young people that you should deal with in your teaching situation is the pluralism in which your junior highs are living. Such multilateral viewpoints bombard your young people not only in the school Monday through Friday but also at the movies on Friday night and at the ball park on Saturday. A generation ago as you sat in your classes at school, the person immediately to your right was Presbyterian, the one ahead of you was Methodist, the one to your left another Presbyterian, and behind you perhaps a Roman Catholic but nonetheless a Christian. While this picture is hardly descriptive of the situation in which every one of us grew up, it nevertheless denotes what it was for the majority of nonurbanites a generation ago, and, to a large extent, it is indicative of a circumstance not far removed from many who dwelt in the city.

Now, however, to the left of your junior high today sits a Jewish young person, in front of him a Jehovah's Witness, to the right a youth who has no religious adherence, and behind perhaps another Christian, but quite likely from another denomination. What causes this situation to be a matter of concern to you is that these young people do not live in a vacuum or simply exist side by side incommunicado. They talk about what they believe and compare similarities and contrast differences. Not infrequently, the result is a questioning by the Christian as to what he believes is the truth. Although such questioning is healthy, provided he receives sound, Biblical answers, a related thought that occurs as a result of his pluralistic environment is unhealthy both to him and to his non-Christian friends, the feeling which has been expressed to this writer in such statements as: "Why get all excited? He's entitled to his beliefs just as I'm entitled to mine. Isn't his religion just as good as mine?" The basic assumption of pluralism is that all truth is relative; there are no absolutes.

As a Christian in this context, such thinking will affect both what and how you teach. Concerning the former, you should often reemphasize the main goals of Christian education, especially the goal in which you are attempting to help your students to develop the confidence and ability to share their faith in response to the Great Commission their Lord gave them. And while not rejecting their non-Christian friends as persons, you are going to have to help your junior high see that the thinking their friends are doing is in direct conflict at certain points with God's Word. Hence, you should plan to study with your class certain units dealing with what non-Christians believe, taking into careful consideration at which specific points they differ and how to respond to those differences.

At this point how you teach will be affected. In order not only to help your students learn what a particular cult believes but also to help them develop the ability to share their faith meaningfully and persuasively with an adherent of such a cult, you will want to use different forms of group discussion, particularly reality-practice and role-play. You will want in undertaking such study to do so in love and concern for others. Such an attitude is imperative for the proper teaching of such units, for it is teaching, nonverbally as well as verbally, the approach of our Lord himself, and it is the best and most effective way to win others to Christ. If you have a judgmental and unloving approach to such subjects, not only will you "turn off" your own students for the most part, but those who adopt your method will not be very effective witnesses for the Lord. Not only will they, by their attitude, be communicating an unloving God (which is just the opposite of what John 3:16 says about the Most High), but they will be forgetting an ancient truth well utilized by Jesus, even though most likely not invented by him: "One will catch more flies with honey than with vinegar." It should be remembered that the honey is referring to the method, not to the message. We do have the responsibility to share our faith, to communicate the whole gospel, and at no time in history has it been more imperative for each Christian to do this than in our age of ever-increasing pluralism.

3

Psychological Development

WEBSTER DEFINES PSYCHOLOGY in the following manner:
"1. The science which treats of the mind . . . in any
of its aspects; systematic knowledge and investigation of
the phenomena of consciousness and behavior. . . . 2.
The traits, feelings, actions, and attributes, collectively,
of the mind; as, the *psychology* of a criminal." Somewhat
more simply stated, what we have here is a twofold description of what is meant by the psychological dimension
of a human being: first, his intellectual aspect, and second, his emotional aspect. We shall consider these two
parts.

INTELLECTUAL

In spite of the fact that scientists claim to be on the
verge of developing a pill within the next fifteen years
that will be able to improve intelligence as well as to
alter it in such other ways as to erase certain memories
and to emphasize certain abilities, it is important that
the teacher of junior high young people have an understanding of the development of the intellectual processes
which influence their ability to think. It is not difficult

to see that a comprehension of how and what a student of a given age can understand, and how this understanding will affect his motivation to behave in accordance with that learning, is not only desirable but imperative in Christian education.

Biblically, man is seen as a whole, a complete oneness. The different parts of man form a unity or totality. Hence, it is fitting that scholars have identified connections among the physiological, sociological, intellectual, and emotional dimensions of a human being's development. Swiss psychologist Jean Piaget has discovered that the ability to think conceptually in abstract operations is a manifestation of mental processes which take place as a result of the maturation of the nervous system and the influences of social environment.[9]

Psychologists have also discerned different stages of development within the intellectual aspect of a person's growth. The thinking in this regard most generally held in highest esteem today is that of Piaget. He sees distinctly different levels of intellectual ability in the age groups *birth through age two,* which he calls the period of sensorimotor intelligence where the infant is learning to coordinate his perceptive and motor functions; ages *two through seven,* which he terms intuitive or preoperational thinking, where the child's understanding is limited to focusing on one aspect of a situation at a time and in which his thought is not reversible, that is, he cannot see an inconsistency and back up to determine a more logically correct progression; ages *seven through eleven,* which he designates as the period of concrete operations where systematic thinking is now observable, reversibility is evident in concrete thought forms, but where there is little extension or generalization from one concrete field to another; ages *eleven through fifteen plus,* which he calls the period of formal operations or propositional thinking, characterized by the capacity to think hypothetically and deductively, logical thinking in the form of abstract concepts, reasoning by implication and ready identification of incompatibility.[10] This latter level is the stage in which our junior high young people are operating during the time they are within our tutelage.

Working from the result of research he had recently completed, Dr. Ronald Goldman developed a schema showing the stages of intellectual growth that is a modification of Piaget's. Noting in his own observations the truth recorded by Piaget, that there is some overlapping between the stages, Goldman found that actually the transition periods are intermediate stages in which rudimentary elements of the next level of operations are being tried, albeit unsuccessfully, and which are providing the necessary experience for the attainment of such skills.[11] While there appears to be only a semantic difference here, as Piaget himself is careful to break down the stage of formal operations into two substages, it is important to notice that there is evidence that no sudden change in thinking occurs with the advent of adolescence. Change does occur from a concrete to a more abstract method of thinking, but it is a gradual change, and the transition takes the form of an intermediate stage of thought processes.

The young person who is beginning adolescence now becomes able to see situations as being either logically true or false, and he can test such propositions to determine their soundness and validity. The junior high is beginning to be able to start with a theory and work back toward the facts, and by the end of the eighth grade he will be able to do this as an intellectual adult. He is able to visualize and to select deductively the one which is the most sound and valid from an analysis of the facts.

His ability to function intellectually is greatly increasing, and as a result everything is coming into question. There are no sacred cows; he is looking very seriously for meaning in life, now that he sees he is becoming an adult, and anything that can't prove its reason for existing and particularly its meaning to him personally, he will feel that he can just as easily do without.

However, his increase in knowledge frequently creates a jumble of ideas that occasionally results in emotional confusion and insecurity. The result of such a state is not infrequently the desire to withdraw into an earlier period which the youth identifies with security and stability. This is perhaps part of the reason why Piaget and Goldman observed that a child doesn't always work at the level of thinking that he has achieved, but performs at different levels in differing subjects or areas, depending upon his experience and how much he has been motivated.

The subject of motivation is crucial in Christian education, and an understanding of its nature and use is imperative. However, as the emotional aspect of the psychological dimension of the human personality also plays an important role in understanding motivation, it is necessary that we deal with it first. Therefore, following the discussion of a few of the implications of the foregoing facts concerning the intellect, we shall turn our attention to the second part of the psychological development of the adolescent young person.

Implications

It has been this junior high worker's experience that youth in this age group appreciate and are drawn to the teacher who takes seriously their growing intellectual ability. The young person who is striving to identify with adulthood over against childhood is very sensitive to any expression by others which he interprets as treating him like a child. Nothing destroys his dignity so deeply as the mortifying thought that he might be mistaken for a child. In a very real way his feelings are justified as well as understandable. What adult would not be affronted by the failure to accord him the proper recognition of a status level he had attained? Therefore, be careful in your teaching to provide questions that are a challenge to a mind which can now think more and more abstractly and which is no longer limited to specific facts. When statements are made, ask the students, "Why?" Press them and challenge them to dig deeply for the answers.

Such intellectual stimulation is vital for another reason. It helps discipline their thinking to be perceptive and thorough in their understanding of as many dimensions as there are to our Christian faith. Such inquiry will better prepare them to deal with the penetrating and profound questioning to which they will be put by a secular world. It is this world to which they have been commissioned to witness (Matt. 28:19–20).

1. *Stretch your students' minds.*

The first implication of the facts of a youth's intellectual development encourages us, therefore, to challenge young persons to press ahead to think hard and deeply. Piaget has cautioned that not to challenge a young person to develop his abilities and to test their limits may cause him to fail to reach his full intellectual capacity. Hence, to fail that challenge would in itself be poor Christian stewardship as well as less than desirable Christian nurture.

    2. *Use methods of teaching in which your students are active rather than passive.*

Since junior high youth are able to think for themselves and no longer need to be spoon-fed, they are now able to function in the much more effective (than, e.g., lecture-type method) discovery, or pupil-participation, technique of teaching. Discovery classrooms become learning laboratories where the young people can apply their intellect to the data available and discover for themselves the truths in God's Word, thereby making it more meaningful to them and retaining what was learned for a longer time.

    3. *Include doctrine wherever applicable in your lessons.*

With the onset of the level of formal operations, the junior high has reached what Goldman calls the stage of readiness for religion; he is intellectually capable of comprehending the concepts of the Christian faith, although he still has a long way to go in his religious search. What this means to those of us who belong to a confessional branch of the church is that we can and should deal with doctrine in the religious instruction of our youth. Since doctrinal learning and the Biblical basis for it should never be separated, doctrine where it applies should be related to every Bible passage being studied.

    4. *Encourage discussion and debate.*

His ability to look beyond the facts now, and the resultant discovery that oftentimes a situation is seen in reality to be neither all black nor all white, creates within the junior high the desire to discuss and debate such issues when he confronts them. Such a method of self-expression not only should be allowed in your class but should be encouraged. Your students will learn more and will strengthen and develop their ability to share their faith.

5. *Be alert for opportunities to minister.*

The force of these new powers, biological, sociological, and intellectual, not to mention emotional, often can leave a young person feeling as though he had been trampled by all four of the defensive linemen of a professional football team. Since he senses the student's confusion, bewilderment, and desire to regress into a past stage of development to escape the agony currently engulfing him, it is important that the junior high teacher be alert for such occasions. Be sensitive to the needs and feelings of each individual in your class so that you can detect any changes in his outward expression. If and when such a change takes place, do not hesitate to speak to that person alone in order to help him work through his struggle. Help him to focus upon the resources he has both on the horizontal plane as well as vertically (loved ones and friends as well as God) which are very real aids through which he can achieve the confidence to continue his growth in the Christian life wherein he can make an important contribution to the world for the edification of God's people and his honor and glory. Such a personal one-to-one encounter is a vital and extremely important part of your teaching ministry. In so doing, you will be creating the context in which the student can discover the limitless depth of God's love and care for him and the strength and confidence flowing from this care which will enable him to find his fulfillment in God's service.

EMOTIONAL

These lines of deep feeling which Matthew Arnold penned for posterity in his famous "Dover Beach" are expressed in different words by thousands of adolescents every day:

> And we are here as on a darkling plain
> Swept with confused alarms of struggle and flight,
> Where ignorant armies clash by night.[12]

As the adolescent strives to emerge from this welter of confusion which exists as a result of the biological changes taking place within him, he senses the need and desire to seek out the opposite of bewilderment: meaning. He wants to realize truth as it relates to him personally; he attempts to understand his own self. He has a new body which, he observes, now possesses new capabilities that have to be integrated into a meaningful self-concept. The identity he had formed of himself as a child is no longer adequate, for it no longer communicates the real him. To be known and loved and to know and love in turn, in fact even to exist at all, a new identity will have to be hammered out in the forge of life.

Although it is true that much time is spent by the adolescent in pondering and contemplating the body and lavishing so much attention on it that mirrors become like magnets, the resultant sexual dimensions of his being which have to be integrated into a meaningful whole in order to form a satisfying self-concept are much more than just physical. As far as the sex drive itself is concerned, there is much evidence that this force is largely psychological in nature. With physical organs that have "come alive" appears a knowledge of their use and the awakening from dormancy of the emotional impulses which accompany that use.

Along with emotional attachment, there is another realm of emotional behavior: the desire for emotional detachment, one form of which is the freedom from parental "domination." This desire reintroduces another aspect of the identity formation: the social. As we have seen in our discussion of the sociological development of the junior high, the individual personality in encountering other personalities in groups becomes modified and refined. The term "identity" entails a continuing feeling of "sameness" with another person or group of persons as though the self were "extended out" to include them, and in which there is a continual sharing of a particular essence of character.

Here again, then, we can see how much it is true that the junior high adolescent is a whole person, a product of all the influences of the different dimensions of his development which bear upon him. Hence, while our discussion has proceeded in fairly neat categories—physiological, sociological, and psychological, and even further subdividing the last into intellectual and emotional—we must, when focusing specifically on one category still deal with the interrelationship of each with the others. For example, we cannot consider the social life of the junior high apart from the physical influences that to a large degree determine his feelings and actions in his relations with others.

At this point you may be becoming somewhat confused and more than a little frustrated, saying, "Wow, I give up!" When you reach this point, you are ready to begin ministering to the junior highs which you are either now teaching or are about to teach, for until you can so grasp the nature of the conflicts they are engulfed with, feeling what they feel, you won't be as effective as you could be in your teaching. To accomplish something you must be relevant, and to be relevant you must deal with these great needs.

Your not-yet-adults, trying to reconcile the physiological revolution from within with the adult tasks facing them from without, are largely concerned with how they look in the sight of others and with the questions whether and how they can develop the ability to fit into the adult world. Hence, if you ask one of your youngsters if he has given any thought to what he would like to do when he graduates from school (do not say "when you grow up," a phrase he feels indicates that the user thinks of him as a child), do not be surprised when he answers intelligently in the affirmative, and not by saying a fireman, a policeman, or cowboy! If he does happen to answer in terms of one of these latter three, it will quite likely be because he happens to know someone personally in such an occupation who is serving as a model for him. Such a task, the establishing of an occupational identity, not only partially meets the need to establish an identity, but also the need to have it be a meaningful one which makes a contribution and is important.

Another emotional dimension that is the result of an interplay between physical and social forces is adolescent love. To a great extent the first love that two young people experience is an attempt to arrive at a definition of their identity whereby each projects an unclear ego-image on the other and through viewing its reflection gradually each comes to see it clarified. This is one reason why you see young couples in a restaurant doing much talking, whereas at a nearby table an older pair with more stabilized personalities, who may be friends of their parents, are hardly saying a word!

As one person expresses himself to another, he can grasp a clearer understanding of what kind of person he is, how well he can think, what his capabilities are, along with the answering of many other questions as he observes the responses of the person with whom he is communicating. It is this understanding for which the young people are striving.

A great fear of young teens is what Erikson describes as role confusion, the direct opposite of an integrated identity. Not to develop an integrated meaning to all the dimensions of life confronting him, and particularly not to carve out a niche for himself in life, is a frightening thought which is the cause of considerable anxiety for a junior high young person.

Another way to deal with this fear in addition to working it out with another in the context of love is to gather with a few more peers in what the adult community calls cliques, in which all persons who are considerably dissimilar (e.g., in skin color, accent, dress) are rejected. Such groups are usually temporary, relatively speaking, and serve the purpose of mutual support which provides a defense against discomfort produced by role diffusion.

Other emotional aspects of the identity crisis include those which come from the great intellectual improvement of the adolescent. The securities of childhood upon which he laid so much faith now seem so completely untenable at times. One of the most impressive of his realizations is the fall from omniscience that his parents have taken.

"How can they be so ignorant?" he may say. "They just *don't understand!*"

In childhood, the Christian youth's religious views were established on basic trust through his parents. He came to know God, because he knew what fatherly love was like. He could trust his mother and father and they told him he must trust God, so he trusted God.

But now adults are seen to be wrong at times—at least Mom and Dad are. They don't have all the answers. "Besides," the adolescent proclaims, "I've never seen God do all these things he's supposed to do, and in my science class I've learned that the world is what it is today because of evolution—and that's been *proved!*" However, as will be seen shortly, the parents' fall from indisputable authority is only a part of the questioning of religion.

The plight of the parent is a sad one. Rarely does he do what is right in the eyes of his teen-age son or daughter. When, in his love for his child, he gives the least impression that he is trying to restore the shackles of childhood, he creates rebellion within the youngster. On the other hand, if he extends the invitation to maturity too quickly, he faces the risk of frightening his adolescent and causing the latter to withdraw into insecurity.

From the young person's point of view, society as a whole isn't much better. It causes restrictions upon him that are tremendously difficult to understand. He is physically capable of becoming a parent, yet he must wait at least a decade in many cases before he can have a family of his own. Almost all sexual activities are taboo to him.

Often he hears an adult make such an unthinking response as, "Oh, it's just another one of those lousy young punks," when one of his peers happened to do something he shouldn't. How many adults realize the personal hurt such a damning remark carves into the very soul of an already confused youth? For a human being who is so desperately searching for uniqueness and acceptance, there could be nothing worse than to be so flushed into the slough of generality.

What, then, does the adolescent do in the face of all this opposition? It seems from his viewpoint that he constantly runs up against obstacles which prevent him from establishing his own identity. There is just no place meant for him in this world. Everybody wants to keep him a baby; even nature won't let him grow up, he keeps getting more and more pimples! This is just one more wall standing between him and the image that he is trying to build.

It is no wonder that episodes similar to these which occur day after day leave many adolescents feeling quite rejected. But then something happens: the youth turns on his foe and takes the offensive rather than the defensive. He begins to disparage everything that he feels is standing in the way of his establishing an identity for himself. He depreciates his parents, the values with which he was raised, and all kinds of social conformity. He goes to extremes to assert and call attention to his individualism. Somewhat ironically he will at the same time conform to the image of the adolescent group with which he most closely identifies himself which is also in rebellion.

But from what exactly is this rebellion? It outwardly appears that he is rebelling against authority figures and values that he feels stand in the way of the achievement of his identity. However, upon closer examination it is seen that he is actually rebelling against himself, or more accurately, what he sees in himself that he doesn't like. It is not so much against authority figures as against his own feelings of immature inadequacies that often are projected on authority figures as well as on others that he is in rebellion against. This is not, however, perceived by the youth.

Many of his anxieties have stemmed from childhood. These, too, will have to be dealt with by the adolescent as he seeks to establish his identity. Much of youth's anxiety is only temporary and will pass with time, as Ann Landers advised her correspondent, but it is no less real. It is often very painful, and while being told often by well-meaning adults that the discomfort is indeed ephemeral, peace seems a hundred years away to the troubled teen.

Thus the teen-ager lives alone. He is a part of but not a full member of two different worlds: the world of childhood and the world of adulthood. He experiences the horror of rejection frequently. It is really no wonder that he often cries out from the depths of loneliness. In his isolation he continues his struggle to find himself and to solve his problems. When he fails at this, the resultant feeling is often one of inadequacy. This causes a further regression, which also has an effect similar to that of anxiety, whereby the individual establishes an identification in a negative way, as a mechanism of avoidance, for the purpose of attaining satisfaction through the achievement of others. This is an unhealthy response to the obstacles in his way. However, there are many healthy ways that adolescents use to work their way through the struggle to find themselves.

Although it is true that the adolescent is living in a state of confusion in two different worlds, he does have a fair idea of what he wants. By "confusion" is not meant what is often connoted by the average use of the term. The adolescent does not wander around in a state of quasi shock; he is not *non compos mentis,* and his lack of a complete identity is not always on his mind. The word "confusion" here simply denotes incomplete integration. While his idea of what he wants is not too well defined, it is slowly becoming clearer. The main thing that is his concern is how to go about achieving a definition of himself as soon as possible.

He has a yearning for meaningful personal experience. He wants to be accepted and understood as a human being in his own right with the amount of dignity which is accorded to that distinction. He wants to be treated as an individual, as one with something to offer that no one else can offer. As yet he's not quite sure what that quality is which sets him apart. But he feels that were he to be accepted as an individual, he'd be able to prove himself.

While faced with this consideration, he is seeking to rediscover himself. He is reexamining all the aspects of himself that have been part of him since childhood. Everywhere he looks he sees change from the way things used to be. In fact he is now a different person. But there is one essential way in which he is the same person, and this will be the basis from which he will be able to establish his new identity in due time. It is the precious element that was cultivated by loving parents and aided by good religious training when he was in the very early years of his life: it is what Erikson calls his basic trust.

What about the youth who hasn't experienced such basic trust because of the absence of such "good religious training" by "loving parents"? Unfortunately, that youth isn't likely to be in your church school class, for the majority of people like him do not find their way into our context—at least historically. However, now with the stress on mission in recent times, you may find such a fellow in your class. Welcome him! It is heartening to note that behavioral scientists do feel that many youths who have not known a healthy basic trust since childhood can still develop sufficient emotional maturity through the help of a teacher who loves, and loves, and loves.

In ministering to the average junior high, you should realize that in time some of his deeply intense feelings will become understandable to him through his experiences. It is quite likely that one special experience at a time will shed light on and magnify a particularly acute feeling on a matter of importance to him. Through that experience he will be able to give meaning to the particularly strong feeling that wells up with him at that point. His feelings about that issue will begin to have some form and structure because of the particular experience.

As these feelings take shape they will present an image that will attract the young person. It will become a symbol for him and have meaning for him in his life. The image will represent what he feels he can become. This is not a completely smooth or free and easy experience, however, for these images also bring to mind all that is in him which could prevent him from attaining this goal. This awareness tends to lead him back into dejection and more conflict. However, the healthy or normal adolescent will not remain dejected but rather will form concepts from these images. These are ideas which concern him and his past, present, and future; his environment, how he feels about it, and how he feels it sees him; and all that has gone into the making of him and what he can become, i.e., his resources. These ideas become the fibers which he will use to weave a realistic and meaningful self-concept.

He develops them by wrestling with them and pondering them. The developed ideas are symbolized in words, pictures, or a combination of both. These are symbols about his ideas which enable him to talk about them and work them through to meaningful fruition.

The adolescent, when he works through this process, will at this point be close to achieving his identity. But, according to Erikson, by this time he will no longer be in junior high school, for the identity achievement process proceeds into early adulthood when, having established a definition of himself, he feels strong enough to fulfill his desire for intimacy in a commitment to concrete relationships with others.

Thus the young teen seeks to establish an integration of all the forces at work without and within him. Such a process has also been described as the striving to achieve a balance between equilibrium and disequilibrium. While the term "balance" adds to our understanding of what the adolescent is trying to accomplish, perhaps the word "integration" is to be preferred for the reason that it best describes the nature of the process more specifically. It denotes the meshing of interrelated dynamics and at the same time connotes the resultant state of equipoise.

Implications

In the light of the foregoing factors in the emotional development of the adolescent, what do these realities indicate ought to be done by you, his church school teacher? We can point out several implications:

1. *Retain natural groupings.*

Use the cliques to your advantage and to that of the young people. As noted above, these cliques are serving a good purpose. Granted, they can serve a destructive purpose, but it can be doubted whether splitting up a clique will hinder the destructive element; you may find that such an action will bring on hostility which will in turn bring on disruptive aggression because you have frustrated a process that was meeting needs. There is also the theological consideration that thereby to produce such a situation in the Christian context is to permit another instance where the method contradicts the message: when the message is that reconciliation and healing through love is possible in the Christian fellowship of believers in Christ, the method of breaking up a clique painfully exhibits the opposite in alienation, rejection, and hostility.

Would it not be far better to use groups that are already meeting needs on the horizontal level, and let them discover through working together in a learning situation in the Christian context a more fulfilling and constructive experience as they allow their thinking and acting to be guided by the vertical dimension in Christ? The method must fit the message.

For those students not in a clique or an ingroup, perhaps you can create a group. Here they will begin to develop a sense of sameness and group consciousness that will help them to meet their identity-forming needs.

2. *Encourage your students to ask questions.*

As you do not allow cliques to threaten you but use them to further everyone's purposes, do the same with the honest questioning that you will encounter from the searching teens. Don't become defensive and feel you have to protect the Christian faith. Be constantly open and frequently encourage your young people to ask any question that is on their minds, even though it may be one that you cannot answer. Do not feel that you are a fount of all knowledge who has to have an answer for every question. Such an image is neither possible nor desirable, for if the young people are really learning, they will be coming up with questions that you can't answer (for that matter, questions that quite possibly no one could answer). Moreover, if you try to see yourself and have others see you as an answer-man, you will again be contradicting what you are teaching by the method you are using. Supposedly, as a Christian teacher, you are pointing to an omniscient God who alone is almighty. If you, without even using words, set yourself up as having all the answers, then you are communicating one of two things: either (1) that you are equal to God or (2) that God has descended to man's level and is now, in reality, a god.

However, if you approach the growing intellectual identity of the adolescent with the expressed feeling that you are mortal, you will not only be nonverbally teaching that God alone is omniscient and almighty but that no question which man can come up with will thwart God and his purposes (Job. 42:2; Prov. 19:21; 21:30–31). You will be communicating a living faith in a living God who acts in personal lives, you will be using sound educational methods as you say, "I'm not sure I can answer all of your question, let's both [or to the class as a whole], let's all try to search out the answer," and you will be providing a real (and Biblically accurate) image of a parent substitute that your students can use as a model while they seek to establish their own concept of themselves.

You don't have to defend God; he can take care of himself. If you do become defensive, you will be communicating that possibly there is something in the Christian message that can be attacked, that it is vulnerable someplace. You may also drive the inquiring adolescent away from the faith by rejecting his natural questioning, something that neither God the Father nor God the Son ever did or does. Christ never turned away an honest question, no matter how sacrilegious it may have sounded. Such an openness served to draw men to him, and you will find the same result in your teaching.

3. *Use young love.*

You need not be threatened by young love. Don't mock it or ridicule it, or try to split up couples either in class or on a class outing. Recognize the purpose such a relationship is serving, and encourage it to serve an even greater purpose by using it. Let such couples make special reports or team teach a particular lesson. Give them the responsibility for a particular aspect of a class outing, such as being cochairmen of the recreation committee or in charge of transportation. You will, again nonverbally, be teaching powerfully the nature and purpose of love and its place in the Christian context.

4. *Help youth become aware of what motivates people.*

Since a youth often is unaware that he is rebelling against feelings of inadequacy in himself which he is projecting on others, refrain from using this little piece of knowledge against him (e.g., "Oh, grow up and stop projecting!") and, instead, use it for him. Do not point out what he is doing in so many words, but try to let him discover it for himself. For example, when a young person cuts down someone else, ask him why he doesn't like that person. When he describes the fault, say, for instance, that the other thinks he's a big shot, ask why it bothers *us* when other people approach us with that air. Then offer a suggestion such as, "I wonder if we don't like that because it sort of threatens us, makes us feel inferior, destroys the conception that we have something important to contribute? And, deep down inside, don't you sometimes feel inadequate, as if you won't make it? I do." Include yourself in such a conversation, because if you make it all other-centered, you will likely turn the teen-ager off, as you, too, will be putting him down, only in a different way, a "nice" way. Also, you will draw your students to you if you share some of your own personal struggles with them. You will not only become real to them and a model they can reach, but you will also be communicating a more realistic message concerning Christianity: faith does not free us from problems but gives us a resource for dealing with them.

5. *Be aware of conflicts that produce the desire for escape, and deal with both cause and effect.*

Be sensitive to your students personally and the difficulties they are encountering. When they become dejected, they may opt for a very human alternative to the situation—they may try to escape. Sex, alcohol, drugs—all provide avenues of escape that many persons use today. The one that an alarmingly large number of junior high youth are selecting currently is drugs, and the number is steadily rising. This problem has become one only in the last decade—not that there has never been a drug problem before the 1960's, but never has it taken on the dimensions it does now, not only in geographical area (being found also in rural communities and parochial schools) as well as social class (drug usage is growing in the suburbs), but also agewise, junior highs and even children having easy access to drugs.

Not only escape but rebellion is a cause for the use of

drugs by teens. Hence, know the conflicts confronting the teen, bring them into your lessons, and use the resources of the Christian faith in dealing with these difficulties.

Have a unit on the purpose of the body and mind and the Christian use of these dimensions of our person. Show films on drugs from the public library, which usually can be rented inexpensively, and invite speakers to your class who are informed on these matters, such as the high school biology teacher or a member of the police department who deals with drugs. Consider also a member of the medical profession who may belong to your church and who could speak from his own Christian frame of reference.

6. *Use the daydreamer.*

If you notice one of your adolescents daydreaming, do not reprimand him for it, for it is also in this way that he is molding ideas into a meaningful self-concept. As his mind wanders from idea to idea, his thoughts are far from idle, for this is one way he is trying to achieve a more mature self. Rather than make him resentful or even teach him that this is bad, why not put his efforts to use in an even more constructive and fulfilling way that will benefit the others in the class also? Include him in discussions, drawing him out about what he thinks and feels concerning a particular subject. Ask him to write a brief paper on a certain subject and share it with the class. Give him a list of subjects on which to write that relate to the unit you are studying and from which he can select the topic that most appeals to him.

7. *Be sensitive to the concerns of the early and late bloomers.*

The shower room before and after physical education class can be a traumatic experience for a young person who is slow in developing physically in comparison to his or her peers. Therefore, be sensitive to the boy who is still very short and to the girl whose breasts haven't yet begun to form while just about all her friends have long been wearing their first bras. Also be careful that in the process you don't reject the girl who is physically mature, or the boy of the same stage of development. One can observe junior high girls walking around outside in the winter with their coats wide open for the obvious reason of allowing their breast development to be observed. If you are a man, be careful to be aware of your motivations. Desiring not to commit the sin of lust in the heart about which Jesus spoke (Matt. 5:27–28), you may find that you are turning away from the physically mature girl when she approaches you, and thus are rejecting her. Again, if you do that, you are communicating something that you do not want to teach: (1) that she or her physical attributes are something to be disdained, or (2) that she should be ashamed of herself in some way, or (3) that it is wrong to take pride (in the right sense) in her body, denying that it is a beautiful gift of God to be used for him, or (4) that God (you are God's representative and the student identifies your feelings with God's) is against sex(uality), or (5) that sex is bad. If you find it difficult to be comfortable in the presence of such a young person, talk with your pastor or a counselor, *but do not reject* that young person because of your hang-up, or worse, project your feelings onto the person (thereby finding yourself saying something like, "She is too interested in sex").

8. *Help your students see unity with Christ as necessary for completing an identity that satisfies.*

This implication is the last which will be considered here, but it is certainly not the least, and depending upon circumstances, is perhaps the most important. Your young people are seeking an identity, so this is the golden opportunity for you to point them to Christ and help them to see that by identifying with him they will complete their identity. By "complete" is not here meant that they will finish building their self-concept and no longer struggle to define where they end and others begin. What *is* meant is that when they appropriate that element into their being, namely, a restored image of God and a healed relationship with God, it will make them what they were intended to be by their Creator and without which they will lack the essence of meaning and purpose as well as the deepest satisfaction in life. Even after accepting Christ as their Lord and personal Savior, becoming one with him, they will still have to tie the strands of the different dimensions of their lives into a meaningful integration, which will take them the better part of a decade. But by accepting Jesus, they will have availed themselves of a very present help for this endeavor, the biggest and most important part of which is now completed.

Conclusion

In Part I we have examined briefly the physiological, sociological, and psychological dimensions of an adolescent's life which exert influences that he is trying to integrate into a meaningful self-concept. We have noted that although there is sufficient uniqueness in each dimension to demand our considering them separately, it is necessary to recognize that there is a great overlapping of the three main areas, and there is a common strand running through them: the attempt to form an identity.

Conspicuous by its absence is a fourth term: the spiritual dimension. Yet the perceptive reader will recall that it is not missing at all, but was visibly evident in our consideration of each dimension.

Biblically speaking, a human being does not have a spiritual segment of his life separable from the other aspects of his total person. Rather, his whole self, everything that he is, exists in relation to God. Hence, his physical, social, and emotional needs will all have importance to you, for they all have theological implications. These three aspects of the young person's life are all dealt with in the context of his relationship to God. Christ is Lord over all of one's life, not just a part (one fourth), and his message speaks to all of a person's needs, not to just one or two. In the teaching ministry we attempt to meet all of a person's needs through Christ our Lord.

Thus we have to begin with a foundation on which to build the ministry, so that it will be able to reach into the very fiber of the existence of the person. Hence, it was necessary for us to find out what those fibers were like so that it would be possible to develop a teaching program that would grasp and strengthen them. Having accomplished this task, we shall now proceed to identify the resources available that will enable us to prepare such a program.

PART II

RESOURCES
FOR PREPARATION

4
Where to Begin Looking for Help

THERE ARE MANY ADDITIONAL SOURCES of information available to you if you desire further knowledge of child development or help in virtually any aspect of education. Many teaching aids are published for secular education which lend themselves to use in Christian education with very little difficulty in transfer. These secular aids should be put to the service of Christian education. God has provided many resources for us on the horizontal level in a variety of fields, including the behavioral sciences as well as education methodology, and he expects us to use them. It would be a poor stewardship of talent to avoid such helps simply because the word "Christian" was not on the package. In the parable of the talents, the wrath of the employer was upon the worker who hid his talent and did nothing with it. It also should be observed that the talent given him was one of the most secular that one can receive—money (Matt. 25:14–30).

1. *Books*

A wealth of good books on child and adolescent development are available today. As observed in Part I, it is extremely important to develop a frame of reference in your own thinking about the junior highs you teach which includes as thorough an awareness of life as they are experiencing it as you can achieve.

2. *Newspapers*

Another secular source of reading material comes right to your doorstep each evening. Many newspapers carry exceptionally good coverage of education news and often contain stories of new methods of teaching that are being used in the schools as well as other helpful thoughts being considered and employed that, with very little effort, you can transfer to your own teaching situation.

3. *Magazines*

A number of fine journals and professional magazines are published for educators. You would do well to subscribe to one, or at least to inform your church librarian of their availability and request that one be subscribed to for all the teachers in the church school. If your church does not have a library, consider it one of your primary tasks to enlist support for a library and then to petition the education committee to recommend its institution.

4. *Library*

If your church does have a library, you have an unlimited number of possibilities educationally. Sign up for a day when you can take your whole class into the library and learn what books are available. Make this tour on the first day you begin a particular unit of study, say on the church. As you go into the library hand each student an outline of the different aspects of the subject that you are going to deal with in class. Under each topic list the books on the church that are available for the junior high age. Then say: "All right, we're going to begin a unit of study on the nature of the church. On the outline you will see the areas we will be dealing with. Now, I'd like each of you to choose an area to be responsible for, and select at least one of the books within that area in which to do some outside reading for extra preparation. When we get to that part of our study, you will be our resource person who has specialized in that subject and will be able to help us think through it." Such an approach not only helps the young person meet some of his needs, such as to be intellectually stimulated, to be seen as unique, different from all others, and to sense that he is making an important contribution, but it also provides you with some extra resources. Moreover, it offers an opportunity for pupil participation in the learning process that is a necessity for the most effective learning.

5. Public-School Teachers and Administrators

There are also a number of resources open to you apart from reading material. Public-school teachers and administrators are usually very willing to offer whatever help they can. Most professional teachers are also willing to have you attend one of their classes as an observer. This opportunity is not only informative but also stimulating and provides many ideas and thoughts that you can use in your teaching context. If you are not already a member, join the P.T.A., where you will encounter still another resource that the schools can provide you.

6. Textbook Committee

Your church school may have a textbook committee. If it doesn't, it would be good for you to encourage the formation of one. It is imperative in this day and age to evaluate regularly the curriculum materials in use in your church school as to whether those you are currently using are the best ones for meeting the needs of your youth. Such an evaluation should be made at least every three years, and your denomination may have forms available which will serve as guidelines to the evaluation of your church school curriculum. If and when your church has such a committee, volunteer to serve on it. Do not be afraid to volunteer for work on such a committee; it is not easy to find people willing to contribute to such a task, and your offer will be most welcome. The publishing companies you will come to know through your service on this committee will offer you much in the way of resources which you can use in your teaching.

7. *Files*

Check to see whether your church has a student file. It may not be open to your free use, due to the inclusion of confidential information, but perhaps the pastor or the director or minister of education, if you have one, will share with you some of the information from the file on the needs of the students you will be having.

The personal resource files and libraries of the ministers in your church are another resource for you. Most ministers gladly loan information from their files on subjects you may be dealing with in your class study.

8. *Students*

Whatever you do, do not fail to utilize the resource right in front of you, your students. Learn from them what their needs are as was discussed in Part I, both by asking them verbally and through writing, and by developing a sensitivity to them and the situations they are encountering in their daily lives. Also, allow your pupils to participate in planning the units you will undertake to study. Have your class elect (or ask for volunteers for) a planning committee to work with you sometime during the week to prepare the following week's lesson. In this way, you will help them understand the reasons why it is important to study certain subjects and they will help you become more aware of their concerns, with which the lessons must deal. The result will be that they will become more enthused and participate more in the class because they have been active in shaping the structure and content of their course of study.

Of course this approach does not mean that the teacher simply abandons his responsibilities to the young people. Nor does it mean that he is no longer teaching. It is a new kind of teaching, a teaching in which the most effective learning is taking place because it is utilizing principles which ensure that when the pupil participates in an active way in the learning process, he will retain more and integrate his insights more meaningfully into his own life situation.

9. *Prayer*

The foregoing are resources that are open to you on the horizontal level. Another resource is open to you, and this one comes from the vertical plane: prayer. Prayer is a resource that is of paramount importance. Through it God can orient your thinking in the direction that will provide the best nurture for your youth, and who knows their needs better than he does? Pray without ceasing as you prepare.

Through prayer the Spirit of God can speak to you and to your students and stimulate you, give you insights that human resources cannot provide, and help you to keep focusing on the basic goals of Christian education as you proceed to prepare your lesson, so that you will not lose sight of your objectives.

5

The Importance
of Establishing Objectives

GENERALLY SPEAKING, the two main goals of Christian
education are: (1) to help children, young people, and
adults develop the ability to share their faith in Jesus
Christ and (2) to help children, young people, and adults
learn to deal from a Christian perspective, with the conflicts and difficulties they will encounter in life utilizing
the resources in faith available to them, so that they will
be enabled to help themselves and others in these situations. Now, how does that statement help you? Well, first
of all, it gives you a broad picture of the general direction
in which you are headed in your teaching experience. It
tells you a little about the general context in which you
will be working and something of the subject matter with
which you will be dealing.

But some very vital factors are missing from the above
statement which are necessary for the communication of
the most relevant and meaningful lesson if those goals
are going to be attained. We have learned that the junior
high needs to be seen as a person in his own right; now,
how in the light of the above statement of goals will he
discover that he is unique and important in God's sight
when those goals group him with everyone else? More-

over, how will you and he know when he has attained those abilities described in the goals? What will the learner be able to do?

Do? Does Christian education deal in behavior that can be measured? Isn't Christian education more the acquiring of a certain amount and kind of knowledge? Perhaps it has often been treated as such, but it was not originally intended to be so, and it should not be so regarded now.

It was the psalmist who asked, "Teach me thy way, O Lord, *that I may walk* in thy truth; unite my heart *to fear* thy name" (Ps. 86:11). The behavioral result of religious education is further described in Ps. 78, where we read that

> God established a testimony in Jacob
>   and appointed a law in Israel,
> which he commanded our fathers
>   *to teach* to their children;
> that the next generation might know them,
>   the children yet unborn,
> and *arise* and *tell* them to their children,
>   *so that they should set their hope in God,*
> and not forget the works of God,
>   but *keep his commandments;*
> and that they should *not be like their fathers,*
>   a *stubborn* and *rebellious* generation,
> a generation whose heart was not steadfast,
>   whose spirit was not faithful to God.
>   (Ps. 78:5–8, italics added.)

In his Great Commission which is the frame of reference for our lives of service for God, Jesus instructs his disciples to be "teaching them to observe all that I have commanded you" (Matt. 28:20). It takes only a cursory glance at the four accounts of the gospel to see these commandments as rooted in action. Immediately after Jesus helped the lawyer discover the great commandment, he proceeded to illustrate what it meant in terms of behavior in the parable of the good Samaritan (Luke 10:25–37). Notice also the educational method that Jesus used with the lawyer. Instead of instructing the lawyer by the lecture method, Jesus allowed the lawyer to tell him. A final example of how the Bible looks at the action aspect of learning is found in James's famous admonition that "faith apart from works is dead" (James 2:26).

We must see learning in terms of behavior change. Simple acceptance of facts is not learning of the quality we are striving to attain in Christian education. What one truly learns affects one's daily decision-making.

A goal, then, is a statement of the broad aim that you hope to accomplish by the end of the course. It is stated in general terms which are open to many interpretations. But something more than a goal is needed in order for both student and teacher to accomplish effectively what has been intended by the goal.

Using as a frame of reference the general goals of Christian education listed above, you as a junior high teacher are going to have to define further more specific goals that you want your young people to be able to accomplish in the time they are with you. You will have to set goals that pertain specifically to them and which will meet the needs discussed in Part I. Then, having set goals that will help *your* students to accomplish the aims of Christian education, you will have to define further not only what you want to do but what you want your young people to be able to do. Such a specific goal is called an objective. An objective is a statement of what the learner will be able to do, the observance of which will let the teacher know that the student has attained his goals.

In determining what the specific needs of your students are, use the information we have already discussed and record it on a sheet of paper arranged like Sheet No. 1 in Appendix A. By doing this, you will have a pretty clear concept of the needs to which you are trying to minister.

The importance of establishing goals directly designed to meet needs cannot be underestimated. In order to fulfill the general goals of Christian nurture, we must ascertain where our students are in their life situations right now. It would be a waste of time to help them learn to deal with needs they are already capable of handling. Young people have frequently chastised the church for answering questions they are not asking, while failing to deal with the ones they are asking. To them, this appears to be a total ignorance of reality which in turn says to them that God isn't very relevant or real. How in such a context can one convince a young person of the providence of God or the Lordship of Christ?

It is also a great disservice to omit preparing our youth for the difficulties of life which, human experience teaches us, they will surely face at one or another point in their lives. We must know their needs in order to know how to approach a particular subject. Is this subject real to them? Are they intellectually and emotionally capable of handling this subject?

In seeking to establish an organizing principle for isolating a goal with which to begin structuring a course or even a unit within a course, the teacher must ask: What are the basic needs of my students that I can deal with educationally? How can I help them to become able to share their faith effectively and to meet their own and others' needs? Having answered these questions, you are now ready to establish some general goals.

Such general goals are stated in terms such as "to know," "to understand," "to believe," and "to grasp the significance of." Such a goal might be worded: "To understand the need to accept one another." This is a valid goal, because it is vital in meeting the needs your youth are facing today and because it is necessary if they are going to witness effectively to others or help them.

But how will you know at the end of your time with these students that they have learned what you are intending to teach them? You must establish several objectives designed to lead to your goal, so that both you and your students can reach the desired end. Unless you communicate clearly just what you want your students to be able to do at the end of your period of instruction, both you and they will be unclear about what is happening. You will not have a definite purpose for the specific things you do (which will result in a poor stewardship of time, and that is a precious commodity in Christian education), the youth will feel that what is happening in their group is meaningless, and neither you nor they will know after the course is over whether they have achieved the goals with which you began. This is one major reason why a great number of teachers throw up their hands in frustration and confess that they "just don't know whether it's been worth it all," feeling "as though nothing lasting has happened to them." The instructor's confusion may well result in the student's confusion and (understandable) hostility.

A well-written objective identifies the desired terminal behavior, that is, those functions which the student should be able to perform by name, specifically, at the end of your course of instruction. The objective should also define the important conditions under which the terminal behavior will be expected to occur, and it should describe how well the student must perform in order to demonstrate satisfactorily his achievement of the skills, knowledge, and/or facts the course intended him to learn. In writing such specific objectives, use concrete terms such as "examine," "write," "identify," and "list," in which the learner is seen as active.

Those characteristics of a Christian education objective which define the terminal or end-result behavior may be described as ones which:

1. Identify specifically the action that will demonstrate to you that your students have achieved the objective.
2. Explain in detail the conditions with which your students will deal in showing that they have attained the objective.

Hence, it is very important to include within the objective what you consider to be a criterion indicating acceptable performance in the terminal behavior. After you have communicated what it is you want your students to be able to do, it will be even better if you can now describe *how well* you want them to be able to do it. You can do this by stating one or more of at least three criteria of acceptable accomplishment.

One criterion is the specification of a *time limit*. The performance of the desired behavior within that time period will indicate to both you and the student what is acceptable performance. Another criterion is the statement in the objective of the *lowest achievement acceptable:* for example, the minimum number of right responses that will be accepted, or the minimum number of principles to be applied, or the minimum number of words to be written. A third criterion is the identification of the *degree of accomplishment* that must be attained: for example, the percentage of correct answers that will indicate mastery of a concept.

Using the above-stated goal, "To understand the need to accept one another," let us try to write some objectives which would help you to communicate that goal in such a way that your students would gain that understanding. In so doing, you will also have a workable model that can be used with other goals. Before you read the following paragraphs, review the past few pages and write an objective, the attainment of which you feel would satisfactorily demonstrate that your students have learned what you intended to teach about this concept.

Begin to establish your objectives by saying to yourself, "I will know that a student has learned [to accept his neighbor] when he shows that he can . . ." In order to tell whether your students have reached, for example, the goal "To understand the need to accept one another," set down possible objectives such as the following: (1) To *examine* the following passages in the Bible: Micah 6:8; Matt. 7:1–5; 22:37–40; and I Cor., ch. 13, *demonstrating* through the methods of discussion and role-play of actual life situations the relationship of these texts to personal acceptance so that given any one of these passages and a life situation, the student will be able to *write* an essay of not less than three pages *identifying* at least three implications in the Scripture for the Christian's responsibility to accept his neighbor. (2) To *identify* the purposes for which we have been created and exist here on earth, *focusing* on that one which is to love our neighbor so that a student will be able to *list* in a five-minute test five reasons why a Christian accepts other people. (3) To *analyze* our motivations in interpersonal relationships so that given a life situation, the student will be able to *identify in writing* his own feelings and *describe* how they help or hinder his acceptance of the person in the situation, and to *list* at least five ways in which he can deal with those feelings so as to be able to accept that person.

SUMMARY

In preparing to teach, you need to identify specifically all you intend to do and what the student must do in order that both of you will be certain he has learned what you were trying to communicate. To compose such an objective, you must first identify the needs of your students, then establish general goals through which those needs can be met, listing specific objectives through which your goals will be achieved.

The way to write these objectives is to follow three basic steps: (1) Identify the terminal behavior the student is expected to perform in order to indicate that he has achieved the objective: for example, the writing of an essay. (2) Define the conditions under which the terminal behavior must occur: for example, that the essay be no less than one page in length and written in no more than fifteen minutes. (3) Describe how well the student must perform the terminal behavior: for example, that he must explain in his own terms at least three points covered by the Heidelberg Catechism in Section III on gratitude.

At first this process of identifying your objectives sounds very difficult and laborious, but persevere. It will come a little slowly at the outset, but after the first few times you will begin to think in these specific thought forms automatically.

Whenever you are tempted to be lax and neglectful in

your preparation of a lesson, think of how you would want the teacher of your son or daughter to prepare. You have been given the important responsibility of the Christian education of God's children. Do not take your responsibility lightly, but in diligence and dedication spend the time necessary to prepare the most meaningful learning experience possible. The preparation of specific objectives will go far in helping you to accomplish that end.

6

The Process
of Classroom Communication

THE DEVELOPMENT OF LEARNING

Retention

An increasing number of statistical studies are being made to determine the way human beings learn. The purpose of such studies is to find those factors which promote the greatest retention with the most facile transfer of learning to believing or acting in the least amount of time. It is instructive to note that a number of the agencies involved in making these studies are industries who want to know how to communicate most effectively to the public that their product is best. The results of their studies should be considered seriously because these companies are staking their bread and butter on the conclusions. Since those results describe the nature and process of learning, and since Christian education also desires very much to know how best to utilize the principles of retention and transfer in order to effect the greatest growth in Christian maturity, it is important that we consider the results of such findings about how learning takes place.

In a study completed by the Socony-Vacuum Oil Company, it was shown that after three hours of the lecture method of communication recall is 70 percent of the original input; after three days the recall has dropped to 10 percent in this method of instruction. In teaching with visual aids only, recall increases to 72 percent after three hours and 20 percent after three days, but when a blend of telling and showing is used, recall jumps to 85 percent after three hours and a very significant 65 percent after three days. The same study shows that 1 percent of our learning comes through the sense of taste, 1½ percent through touch, 3½ percent through smell, 11 percent through hearing, and 83 percent through sight.[13]

Another study, corroborating the Socony findings, adds two additional facts: a learner retains approximately 80 percent of what *he says* and approximately 90 percent of what *he does*.[14] Hence, these two studies conclude that all of our senses aid in increasing our learning.

This insight is, however, not entirely new. The Bible contains many accounts where all five senses are used in the learning process (Deut. 4:28; 6:4; I Sam. 14:29; Matt. 13:16; John 20:27). God has from the beginning used all of our attributes as channels through which he could communicate with us. In fact, regarding visual aids, God has spared nothing to use as a medium through which we could learn. All creation has been used by God for our instruction (Ps. 19:1–6; Rom. 1:19–20).

We have already seen that learning is directed toward the goal of behavioral change. Having postulated that, it is possible to identify at least six principles for facilitating the learning of concepts. Since the junior high young person is now becoming intellectually capable of comprehending concepts, these six steps will be most helpful in the adolescent's acquisition of doctrinal (conceptual) knowledge in such a way that it will become an influence in his life.

1. *Organize the concept into pertinent divisions for learning.*

There are basically three dimensions to consider when organizing material into units for study: difficulty, length, and relationships.

When preparing a lesson, proceed from easier to harder concepts. For instance, when learning about the covenant relationship between God and man, deal first with such basic concepts as family, authority, and responsibility.

Give serious consideration to the amount of material you want to deal with in your class situation. If you give your students too much to learn at any one time, they will lose the opportunity to search and explore for meaning in what they are studying. Hence, they will learn a great deal less, since pupil participation is essential to meaningful learning which issues in retention and transfer (behavior change). The principle of length also has implications for how you handle the textbook itself. Plan to spend more time on longer units of study; don't spend the same amount of time on each lesson regardless of the subject. For example, don't take a chapter a week of your text automatically, even though one chapter is five pages long and another is twenty; spend more time on the twenty-page chapter. There may be exceptions: for instance, the five-page chapter may be dealing with a subject that your students are having a harder time grasping than a subject that comes easier to them in a longer chapter. If so, you should spend more time on the one that is more difficult. Your youth are individuals and should be considered as such. Your next class may have no such trouble with the subject which perplexed this year's group.

Group material with regard to relationships. When studying about the Trinity, learn separately first about the Father, then about the Son, and finally about the Holy

Spirit. Next discuss the interrelationships of the Three Persons as a whole, as Trinity. By so grouping this material the relationship between each part to the whole can more easily be understood and better learned.

2. *Encourage and advise your students to do individual work.*

Studies have shown that students who have been given an opportunity to discover the truth of a concept through actively searching attained a more thorough understanding of the concept and remembered it better.[15] This is also a method of teaching which creates interest and stimulates the desire to learn more.

3. *Simulate life situations that illustrate the concept.*

When teaching the concept of forgiveness, for example, don't simply tell students what it is and then study a few verses from the Bible that touch on the matter. Set up a situation wherein your students can deal with the matter realistically. Using a method such as reality-practice grouping, have your students role-play a real-life situation that they might well encounter. Have them deal with it in such a way that they must relate their Christian belief directly to the situation at hand. In this way they not only are learning about forgiveness existentially but they are also learning about how to witness. This is a cardinal rule in Christian education. We cannot teach about principles in the classroom and expect that our students will automatically be able to perform with 100 percent efficiency when they all of a sudden encounter such a situation in their daily lives. The classroom must be seen as a laboratory workshop in which the Christian can prepare for the realities that will confront him perhaps even before he leaves the building. Such realities may often occur right in your class, and you should deal with them on the spot. For instance, if a discipline problem erupts, you have a tremendous opportunity to deal with the nature of sin as well as of forgiveness. At this point you will also be teaching much about how God relates to us through Christ.

There will be some concepts that will be impossible to teach through experience: for example, God, omnipotence, eternity. Do everything you can, however, to help the learner to grasp the meaning of such concepts. Visual aids will help with such principles that cannot be experienced, but the main point here is that one cannot simply give conceptual transfusions to someone else. Each person must achieve understanding for himself.

4. *Provide a simple and clear definition of the concept.*
This is a principle which cautions against a possible misuse of the preceding emphasis on learning by doing. Certainly doing is imperative if learning is to occur, but it cannot be the sole means through which retention and transfer are expected to be effected. It is important that hard thinking take place before, during, and after the experiential dimension of the learning process occurs. Simply being involved in a lot of activities in the classroom does not mean that a concept will be learned, for experience must be formulated intelligibly in words if an effective witness is to take place. Although it is true that we witness with our actions as well as with our words, the Bible nowhere indicates that the former is more important than the latter or even that it should take place without the latter.

If one of the two main goals of what we do in Christian education is to learn to share our faith in response to our responsibility under the Great Commission, then we must also develop the ability to verbalize our experience with God through Christ who has told us that we are to go forth and teach all that he has commanded. The word "teach" as Jesus used it carries the connotation in Greek of verbal proclamation. Many people, desiring to avoid either the uncomfortable rejection which might happen if they spoke of Christ (Matt. 10:16–22) or the responsibility of developing the ability to express their faith verbally, think that witnessing through living a good life is enough. This attitude must be discouraged in your class, for such witness could point to Buddha or to Muhammad as well as to Christ, and it is our task as Christian teachers to make sure that all we do points to Jesus as the subject of our witness. It cannot be one way or the other; it is not an issue of either/or but of both/and. Verbal as well as nonverbal witness is imperative, and we must seek to develop our students' ability to perform both, for the latter without the former is meaningless, and the former without the latter is incredible.

5. *Identify the practical implications of the concept for daily life.*

Be constantly looking for examples to which you can point as illustrations of how what is being learned relates to life as your junior highs are living it. Check the film catalogs of audio-visual supply houses, and do so regularly, for new films are continually being produced that are of excellent content and that help greatly to enable your student to visualize how what he is learning relates to his life situations.

6. *Help the student evaluate his understanding of the concept.*

This principle not only contains the valid educational method of reinforcement which further strengthens and sustains what has been learned but it also teaches a valid theological truth which is Biblically sound, namely, that man is limited, fallible, and imperfect. He is not God, and it is good to reevaluate what has been done in order to determine whether further improvement is necessary. Moreover, evaluation provides man with an aid to the development of self-discipline and growth in responsibility.

As a tool for learning, testing is a good approach to use. As the test form of evaluation will be dealt with later, we will not consider it further here. Another means of evaluation is the review, both orally in discussion of specific questions and through the acting out of a situation in such a method of group interaction as role-play.

What should not be used in evaluation, however, is the practice of memorization as a method of learning concepts. Memory work is a sound and valid method of learning for children of a certain age, but with the intellectual capabilities of the junior high, it is poor stewardship of God's gifts and it is scorned by junior highs themselves, who interpret this method as an adult's nonacceptance of them. Moreover, this practice with the teenage group does not ensure the learning of the meaning of the concept that is committed to memory.

Contrary to a belief widely held in evangelical circles, memorization is not synonymous with reinforcement. It has been shown that reinforcement (e.g., "Good work, Jan") will increase the probability that the student will repeat the act, increase his activity, his pace, and that his interest in learning will be heightened.[16] Yet it has also been demonstrated that rote learning does not issue in as good an understanding of concepts or in the retention of them as does the discovery method of learning.[17] In addition to these findings, it should be remembered that the negative feelings of the junior high to rote learning will, if he is forced to learn in this manner, result in wrong impressions regarding the free will of man under the providence of God. Furthermore, there is more than a good chance that he will reject this learning. Our youth are "all highly resistant to indoctrination from outside the youth subculture; . . . education allows the individuals to make the discoveries while indoctrination forces information and beliefs on others." [18] Our young people are no different from us; we, too, are not eager to gag on concepts that are shoved down our throats.

These, then, are the general principles which, if followed, will greatly aid you in communicating concepts to your students in such a way that they can retain them and meaningfully incorporate them into their life situations. But now the question arises, How does one motivate his students to want to learn these concepts?

Motivation

Motivation is basic to learning. We can have the best textbooks, the greatest catechism, and the newest curriculum, but if we cannot excite the young people to roll up their sleeves and dig into it, learning will not take place. This reality also applies to the most important book of all in Christian education, the Bible.

It has been found that it is not so much familiarity with the Bible's content as an attitude toward the Bible that leads to an increased interest in religion.[19] This means that it is imperative that you as their teacher exhibit an attitude which communicates that you feel the Bible is an integral part of your life. By establishing an atmosphere in which the Bible is held in high regard, you will help your students to begin to pick up the same feeling.

Here are several suggestions that will aid you in creating student motivation.

1. *Help your students focus on the goals being sought.*
In order to accomplish this end, you should employ the use of a variety of instructional materials, for such teaching aids help to focus attention on what is being learned. (Remember the statistical evidence noted above which indicates the increased retention through employment of more than one sense.)

2. *Encourage natural curiosity.*
You will find that frequently your youngsters will start off on digressions, and before you know it the class is discussing a subject that only remotely if at all touches upon what you had intended to teach. This is not necessarily bad. The key which will tell you what to do when you realize that you are in such a situation is whether or not the digression is meeting a need. If you sense that it is only a diversionary tactic to avoid undertaking a responsibility, then gently say something like, "Well, group, let's return now to the subject at hand before we wander too far astray." However, you are much more likely to find that the digression is dealing with a need that the youth feel and is directly related to one or more of the forces, discussed in Part I, which influence them. In such a case, *it would be wrong to divert them* back to the original subject *at this time.* There is always plenty of time to return to the point at which you started, but there may never be another occasion when you can deal with a certain need opportunely and while they are highly activated. Remember what Jesus did when, while he was preaching, four men lowered a paralytic down through the roof so the man could be healed. Our Lord did not

say, "Take him away, you're interrupting me; I have to finish my lesson." Not at all! Rather, seeing that a need had arisen, he stopped what he was doing and dealt with that need. Furthermore, he used the incident to make a point in his teaching. Such an example we can well afford to follow (Mark 2:1–12).

3. *Encourage existing interests.*

The 3″ x 5″ card approach mentioned above, through which you can ascertain needs, provides a medium for finding interests. Even suggesting that their choice will be used in organizing what they study will in itself be a motivation to interest in the class. As you come to aspects of your study to which the special interests of the young people relate, ask a particular person if he will do a special report on that part of the subject.

Interest grouping is also an effective tool in inducing motivation. When you begin to deal with a subject that is rather broad (e.g., salvation), divide it up into subsections of related but smaller subjects. Then let your youth select the subtopic they would like to work on, and form task groups which do special study in those areas and report back to the large group.

4. *Use individual rewards only if absolutely necessary.*

Great care must be exercised in giving rewards. This suggestion contains many dangers, and this is especially true in Christian education, where there is less stress on the need for competitive and tangible success. A person can sustain great emotional hurt when he fails in the sight of his peers. Interpersonal competition, furthermore, creates distinctions and undermines bonds, real or potential, between people. And all this is just opposite of what is being attempted in the Christian nurture of the healing community, the people of reconciliation. The second of the two major goals of Christian education is to develop the ability and the sensitivity within people to meet each other's needs; interpersonal competition is I-centered, whereas this goal is other-centered.

Moreover, rewarding one child is in itself punishing others. Programs of rewards favor young people of families that attend faithfully, or who have a high I.Q., or who receive much parental support. Is the young person who has a more intelligent mind or a more outgoing personality, and who can come up with more correct answers more times than another person, necessarily a better Christian?

Yet, studies have shown the powerful effect that rewards have upon the motivation to learn.[20] It has been shown that the verbal reward is less effective in stimulating one to learn than concrete rewards.[21] Is it not better to give a reward and retain interest in the subject being studied?

Perhaps it is possible in dealing with the matter of competition and rewards as a method of motivation to develop a set of helpful guidelines which take into consideration all the above pros and cons. (a) First of all, use this method only *if necessary*. Try all the others first. Many teachers ignore the deeper levels of motivation and employ a program of rewards right off the bat. It is very possible that you will not need to use this method for motivating your students to learn if you try the others first. This writer has not had to use it in order to stimulate students to learn, but has found that the discovery approach to learning in itself was enough to motivate. (b) If, on the other hand, the reward method is needed, *tell the students very clearly that they are competing with themselves and not with each other.* Have competition, but let each class member be in competition with himself and not with the others in the class; let him clearly understand that he is to try to do better than he did before (e.g., that he is to do better on this test than on the previous one). Then be sure you rate their progress in relation to what they have accomplished previously and not in relation to what the others have done. (*c*) When you give tangible rewards, make sure that each member of your class receives the same thing. The key to effectiveness is that they won't all receive rewards at the same time, but psychological damage will be averted by the fact that each *will* receive the reward when he does better than he has done in the past. For the best results, tell them this before they begin the task, since it has been demonstrated that it is the promise of such a reward rather than the reward itself which constitutes the motivating stimulus. (*d*) Keep the rewards small, and don't use this method too often. If you employ this device primarily in the early phases of your course of instruction, quite possibly your students will associate the joy of the reward with doing the task. Moreover, this favorable experience is later identified with the feeling of accomplishment which becomes a motivating drive and eliminates the felt need for rewards.

5. *Make assignments at the skill level of your students.*
Be sure that tasks and material are neither too easy, which will produce boredom and hostility (the former for obvious reasons and the latter because of the uncomfortableness of boredom and because it will be interpreted by the junior high as treating him as a child), nor too hard, which will produce anxiety. Follow the implications

of the increased intellectual level of the junior high adolescent.

6. *Choose goals equal to the skill level of your students.*

This principle has implications for Christian education especially if you have students who are slow learners. By communicating with their parents, you can in a general way develop a fairly accurate understanding of the limitations of each and determine to accept a lower level of attainment for them, so that they don't experience constant failure or too facile achievement of simplistic goals. The important factor for Christian education is that the student grow toward the goals for which he is striving, the better to share his faith and the better to meet human needs, *not* that he grow as much as another person.

7. *Help your students evaluate their progress toward achieving their goals.*

Discuss with your class what they feel should be a goal worthy of attainment in your unit of study as you approach the midway point. Say, for instance: "I feel it would be good for us to evaluate where we are and use a test as a guide for that evaluation. Then, at the end of our study of this unit, we will have another evaluation in order to measure our growth. How about if we say that by next week when we have our evaluation you should be able to identify these concepts and be able to relate them to a given life situation [give each a list of the concepts], and by the end of the unit you should be able to do the same with these [another list, which includes the first list plus others to be studied next]? Can you handle this task?" Since the test will be subjective, and since you know the members of your class individually, personally, you will be able to help them through meeting with them on a one-to-one basis to determine what is acceptable growth for each.

8. *Keep tension at the proper pitch.*

It is important to recognize that too much tension produces disorganization, anxiety, and resultant inefficiency. For a student to want to achieve a goal (e.g., the learning of the concept of forgiveness), there must be a challenge, that is, an awareness of a discrepancy between what is and what can be. Your task, then, is to help him discover that discrepancy and help him to focus on the attainment of the future state. However, do not make it so difficult for him to perform required tasks that he begins to become frustrated, for the result will be not only disorganization and inefficiency, but it is very likely that he will give up and become apathetic. Keep in mind that when one does something that produces pleasure or enjoyment, there is a usual tendency to repeat it. If you can provide a number of such steps along the path of the learning process, your student has a very good chance of grasping what you hope he will.

9. *Draw upon your students' families for help.*

It has been determined that the family plays not only an integral but a primary role in motivating its youth to faith. "Researchers reveal that motivation is dependent upon the attitudes of pupils to religion and to the subject of religious teaching in church and school. This is further dependent upon the attitudes of the pupil's family, and especially of his parents." [22] This is a frustrating truth for a teacher, for it places a crucial element of the issue of motivation outside his reach.

Yet, you can still do much to exert a good deal of influence, even though the parents do play such a crucial role. This writer has found that communication between the teacher and the parents has a positive effect upon the student's response in the classroom situation. Many parents are simply unaware of the important function they have and the contribution they can make, and they feel good about knowing that they are very much needed in the Christian nurture of their children. In many cases it is simply a process of adult education that can be accomplished if you meet and talk with them, encouraging them to become involved. If they have a regard for the Bible, share with them the references mentioned above which indicate that they have the primary responsibility for the Christian nurture of their children, that your ministry is supplemental to what they are doing, and that your effectiveness is greatly minimized without their help. Then indicate that this help involves a continual interest in what their children are doing in church school to the extent of helping them with homework. It also means a much more difficult task: to communicate to their children an attitude toward Christian education that indicates the exciting possibilities it holds. At this point you may have to show the parents why Christian education *is* important, and the best way to begin is to tell them how it helps you.

Of course, there will be some parents who will still refuse to follow through on their share of the responsibility of providing Christian nurture for their children. Since this is in clear violation not only of Biblical precepts but also of their congregational (and in Reformed faiths, parental) vows at baptism, the problem now becomes a judicial matter, and you should take it to the elders of the church. Simply mention the case(s) to an elder and ask him to bring the subject before the attention of the judicial committee. This may seem difficult to do, yet bear in mind that it is in the best interests of the young person you are trying to nurture that you do this.

Pupil Participation

Thus we have found that learning is greatly developed and motivated by student involvement. Furthermore, we have found that pupil participation does not compromise our goals in Christian education, but greatly increases our chances for their attainment.

At the point where we begin to create learning experiences in which the pupil can enter in order to discover the truth for himself and that will enable him to express himself, we are not only approaching the goals toward which we are striving, but we are also meeting the basic needs he is encountering. As we learned in Part I, all the different dimensions of life that he is experiencing present strands that he must weave together in order to form a meaningful personal identity. When he becomes involved in the learning process as an active participant rather than as a passive observer, he is more able to integrate all the viable elements of the faith which have come alive through making the classroom a living laboratory of life. Moreover, he can thus make a personal identification with what is being learned, for the concepts he is studying are no longer objective stereotypes but subjective realities. God is no longer a three-letter word on a page but a Living Force who operates through other persons and also directly. This "living into" should be the basic method, the starting point of our approach to teaching. If the lecture approach is used, it should be incorporated into the framework of the participation context;

the participation context should not be pieced into a basic lecture framework.

Just as we found that the Bible treats man as a whole, psychiatrists today tell us that we must, in attempting to change ourselves for the better, deal with the emotional as well as the intellectual aspect of our being, for the emotional not only has a great effect on our perception of ourselves, our identity, but it cannot be controlled by the intellectual aspect, and must therefore be dealt with directly in the learning process. Hence, the active involvement of pupils in the classroom situation makes possible a learning that is nonintellectual as well as rational.

Long before the advent of psychology as a discipline in itself, the Reformers recognized the importance of the nonintellectual dimension of Christian nurture. Writing in the sixteenth century, John Calvin defined faith as "a firm and certain knowledge of God's benevolence toward us, founded upon the truth of the freely given promise in Christ, both revealed to our minds *and* sealed upon our hearts through the Holy Spirit." [23] Calvin saw that God ministers to us intellectually ("to our minds") as well as emotionally ("sealed upon our hearts").

A few years later the Reformed churches of the Palatinate recognized the need for a catechism that would express their faith. The writers, Zacharias Ursinus and Caspar Olevianus, defined that faith as "not only a certain *knowledge* by which I accept as true all that God has revealed to us in his Word, but also a *wholehearted trust* which the Holy Spirit creates in me through the gospel." [24] In striving to attain our goals in Christian education, we must, therefore, employ methods that are designed to nurture the emotional as well as the intellectual aspects of our adolescents' personality. If they are to shape their faith, they must first develop a faith to share, and since faith is not merely intellectual, means other than intellectual ones are going to have to be used to communicate the concept of faith.

As a teacher, you are going to have to do more than tell a student that he should have faith. You will have to create the circumstances in which he can begin to experience faith and its attributes, e.g., security, acceptance, and community. One way to go about establishing such circumstances is to work toward building a group consciousness wherein your class comes to see itself as having a group identity different from that of the local Boy Scout troop or a Camp Fire Girls club. Help them to establish a climate of trust and acceptance wherein each can experience such a reality. You will have to begin with yourself, accepting each of your students just as he is, without requiring that he act or dress in a certain way or say certain things before you will give him love. Using your attitude as a model, you can work toward helping the class members to accept one another. Gradually, as experiences arise you can relate them to the students' relationship with God. For example, if John pokes Mary and you see it, you could stop and deal with the matter by discussing the dynamics of the situation—what motivated John's behavior and how Mary feels. Then ask Mary how she feels toward John, whether she can accept him. If she can, ask John how he feels about Mary's acceptance of him *in spite of* what he did. The relationship to God's love for us is obvious and by *asking* (not telling) whether anybody can point it out, much growth by discovery will have occurred.

The ancient distinction between "head" knowledge and "heart" knowledge and the emphasis on the need for both is still valid. A student who has only "head" knowledge will neither reach the goals of Christian education himself nor be able to convince anyone else of their worth, for as we learned in our consideration of motivation, learning is dependent upon motivation, which is predicated upon a desire for something, and desire is an emotional response, not an intellectual attribute.

Transfer

Hence, for the pupil to be able to relate what he has learned to his situation and in such a way that he can express it to others, he has to begin to develop these relationships while he is in the process of learning. He has to make what he is learning real to himself, and for him to be able to do this, the classroom has to be turned into a learning laboratory.

There are at least four principles that will facilitate the transfer of learning which are valid for your teaching situation.

1. Accent Biblical truths that readily relate to personal experience.

Transfer is the process of using what has been learned in dealing with different situations with greater effectiveness. Therefore, the first principle requires concentration on basic Biblical truths that can be related directly to life situations. Stress such subjects as sin, love, forgiveness, service. Don't dwell on the more academic topics such as election, angels, church history, the nature of heaven, and the kings of Israel. This comment does *not* mean to avoid teaching these subjects. The key word is "dwell." Do not *dwell* on such subjects, and certainly don't spend as much time on them as on those in the former group. When these subjects are dealt with, try to relate them directly to the life situations of your students.

2. *Employ realistic generalizations.*

Use your teaching situation to try to help your students build a frame of reference rather than to try to give them an answer to every question they will face. Obviously this latter approach is unrealistic. Especially in ethical situations your students will encounter areas where absolutistic answers are undesirable. For preparation for the gray areas of life, help your students to construct a meaningful and integrated viewpoint that will enable them to analyze a situation in the light of Biblical principles. You do not want them to act as computerized robots searching for the IBM card on which the component parts of an ethical decision have been programmed, but as individuals having a frame of responsibility and the loving desire to serve, cognizant of sinfulness and limitations, yet relying on the Spirit of God to guide them to the best solution. As is readily apparent in this example, the "answer-man" approach is impossible because of the teacher's inability to foresee every situation that the student will encounter. Yet it is amazing how many well-meaning teachers this writer has met who do try to answer every question in their teaching, the end result of which is frustration and insecurity on the student's part and an inability to cope with the large number of situations one meets in life.

3. *Help your students to draw parallels.*

In studying about the concept of forgiveness, for instance, present an example of a life situation and ask the student to tell what he would do in this situation in the light of what he had just learned about forgiveness. Have the student tell you what he would do in the situation; don't tell him what he should do.

4. *Help your students evaluate their skill in applying
   principles to new circumstances.*

Through such methods as written and oral testing, role-
play, and some of the other techniques desired in Part
III, you can present your students with new situations at
different points throughout the study of a unit on a particular concept and record their response. Note how they
do at the beginning of a unit on acceptance, for instance,
then how they react at about midpoint, then at the end.
In this way, using the example of acceptance, you can
determine whether your student has grown by midpoint
in his ability to demonstrate acceptance in comparison
with how he reacted in his test situation at the beginning.
Of course, it is important to share the results with the
student and let him share in the evaluation of the outcome
so that he can see what he needs to do to improve.

The Importance of Relationships

We have seen the tremendously important role that
pupil participation plays in a student's learning process.
We have also noted that he senses how God deals with
man through how you relate to him. Putting these two
important aspects of the classroom situation together, we
have before us perhaps the most valuable of all means of
Christian education in the church school: the interpersonal relationship between teacher and student. In fact,
Christian teaching is impaired over an extended period
of time (beyond the length of an elective course) without
a personal relationship between teacher and student.
It is very desirable that the teacher come to know each
pupil in an environment other than the Sunday school
classroom. He must know his student's interests, skills,
doubts, fears, and joys.

In the eyes of your students you are God's emissary. You are his representative, and the way you deal with your students is the way they perceive God dealing with themselves. It is as they experience your acceptance, care, and firmness in a context of love that they will be able to comprehend their relationship to God through Jesus Christ, which is necessary for reaching the first goal of Christian education.

You are working with young teens who are attempting to build an identity, and it is important that you keep in mind the fact that their self-concept is formed both *of* and *by* the reflections of other people toward them as individuals. Their self-concept will not be complete until you help them solidify it in Jesus Christ, for it will have to be through your person that they discover God's message to them. The simple reading of the Bible in class is usually not enough for young people to understand the message of God's Word to man. A student recognizes and acknowledges the Bible to be the Word of God and true when he sees that someone significant to him truly believes what the Bible says and when the message of the Bible comes to life through that person.

He sees the message of acceptance, care and firmness in the context of love which God has for us become a reality in his life when he can experience it in the laboratory workshop of life which is his classroom. As the student perceives and accepts this message for himself, you must then be instrumental in helping him to evaluate his relationship to the others in the class. As Jesus taught in his summary of the law, the love of God goes hand in hand with the love of neighbor (Matt. 22:37–40), a necessary response to the loving God and also an important element of attaining self-understanding or identity.

At this time, you should be helping the class learn to relate to one another as the church. Deal with all the experiences they encounter. For instance, if you sense strained relations between two or more, and you have been meeting as a group for a while so that a sense of "groupness" is beginning to take place, bring the hostile situation out before the whole group. This will not be easy to do, because we have a natural desire to sweep strong feelings under the rug. Yet in so doing, we teach something very unbiblical regarding the nature of the church and its task in the world. Instead of teaching by example as well as by word that the church is a healing community of reconciliation, we are teaching at least by example that it is a place (instead of a people) that allows for the perpetuation of alienation and hostility.

The process of classroom communication is greatly affected by the interpersonal relationships of the young people we are trying to teach. We will not be able to help our youth learn the Biblical truths concerning man's reconciliation with God and man's reconciliation with man unless we begin *right in the learning situation* to live out in life what we are learning in concept.

Through interpersonal dialogue right in the classroom, experiences can be provided that will mold an adolescent's living concepts of the nature and mission of the church, his view of himself and of how he relates to that church and to its God. Therefore, spend time in working with the relationships within your group. Supply opportunities wherein your young people can come to know each other as persons of worth and value because of their relationship to God through Christ. If tension arises within the group, bring it out into the open and talk it through. If one youth punches another, say something like, "I sense that you're a little angry because John slugged you, Bill. Just how do you feel?" Then try to find out why John did it. After the motivations are out in the open, try to help Bill extend himself in forgiveness to John and thereby to accept him. In such ways, help the class to transfer this action both as an example of the kind of love and acceptance God has for us who have wronged him, and as the response of gratitude to him who has so accepted us, even though we do not deserve it. In such ways you will be teaching more about the truths of the gospel in fifteen minutes than you could in a year of lecturing.

The Role of the Teacher

From what we have learned in this chapter regarding the process of classroom communication, particularly about how learning takes place, a number of implications are directed toward the role of the teacher, and since these implications denote some functions of the instructor that are rather different from those that have been accepted in times past, it is important that we consider this subject. Perhaps the most important element in the image you have of yourself as a teacher (which you should have firmly established before you entered the classroom) is that you are an example, one who tries to "practice what he preaches," but not an example of perfection. Rather, you are an example of a person who admits and feels sorry for his sinfulness, but who is also conscious of the fact that he is completely forgiven and cleansed of that sin by the grace of Jesus Christ. And you should not hesitate to admit, as did the apostle Paul, that you still struggle with your "old" man (Rom. 6:6 [KJV]; 7:7 to 8:1). The identity-forming adolescent who is searching to understand why he "does the very thing he hates" will not only be greatly comforted and intrigued to hear this, but you will in the process become more real to him as will the God with whom he can identify.

You are also one who creates a context or climate wherein the student is stimulated to grow in his understanding of what he believes and so can develop the confidence and ability to share what he believes with others. Such a teacher attempts to encourage student participation, recognizing that growth takes place best when the learner becomes involved in the learning process, wherein the class members are encouraged to discover for themselves the truth of the subject being studied and then to share their understanding of that truth with others.

You are one who is seeking to further his own growth with that of his class, one who wants to grow with them. You are not an answer-man, a fount of all knowledge, a person who doesn't need to grow any more and who doesn't make mistakes. You, like Paul, recognize the need for growth as long as you continue in this phase of your life. "Not that I have already obtained [the resurrection from the dead] or am already perfect; but I press on. . . . Straining forward to what lies ahead, I press on toward the goal for the prize of the upward call of God in Christ Jesus." (Phil. 3:12–14.)

These are the main ways in which your identity as a Christian teacher differs from that traditionally held not only by people who think they know what a teacher should do but also by many teachers themselves. However, included within your own realized self-concept should be many of the traditional elements of "teacherness," most notably: one who knows why he is teaching, who has a purpose; one who has planned carefully ahead of time what he wants to do in a particular class session, even though he doesn't accomplish all he sets out to do. He is always present before the session begins; he is committed to Christ and endeavors to be Christlike in his own life and loyalty to the church; he is a *friend* to his pupils, taking a personal interest in each one. He loves all his young people so much that he has a desire to enter into their situation (though not losing his own identity) where he can be a guiding influence through which Christ can work. He has something of the same feeling that Holden Caulfield described to his sister Phoebe when he said:

Anyway, I keep picturing all these little kids playing some game in this big field of rye and all. Thousands of little kids, and nobody's around—nobody big, I mean—except me. And I'm standing on the edge of some crazy cliff. What I have to do, I have to catch everybody if they start to go over the cliff— I mean if they're running and they don't look where they're going I have to come out from somewhere and *catch* them. That's all I'd do all day. I'd just be the catcher in the rye and all. I know it's crazy, but that's the only thing I'd really like to be.[25]

7

If You Are Team Teaching

Since there is an increasing trend today toward organizing large groups for instruction, there is a good possibility that you may soon find yourself in a team teaching situation. If you are not now teaching as a member of a team, you may wish to examine the possibilities of such an opportunity, for having both used the method and introduced others to it, this writer has found that there are not only a number of advantages to team teaching, but once one has experienced this approach the usual response is the desire to continue in it. Some teachers have even expressed the feeling that they will never again teach alone.

In preparing for a lesson, we find that all the principles which we have considered above apply to team teaching as well as to individual teaching. However, a number of other principles apply especially to the team approach, and these will be the focus of this chapter. Before exploring them let us first seek to understand just what is meant by the term "team teaching."

Generally speaking, team teaching is instruction that is based on the relationship between two or more teachers who work cooperatively with a class. Each teacher has a particular responsibility for special parts of the class activity; there is a division of labor.

But why do we employ this technique of teaching? First of all, it is nothing new. Jesus and the early church used teamwork in their educational-evangelical efforts. When Jesus sent out the Seventy on their mission, he sent them two by two (Luke 10:1 ff.). In Acts, ch. 15, we read of the mission teams of Barnabas and Mark and of Paul and Silas working together (Acts 15:39–40).

Yet there are further reasons for the use of this method of teaching, the recognition of which undoubtedly led the New Testament church to employ this means of instruction. We recognize that there are important and significant differences among teachers. We differ in strong points, talents, skills; we differ in interests; and we differ in experiences. Why not combine these strong points into a unified and expanded stewardship of teaching talent?

We must also recognize that there are important and significant differences among the students in any given class; some learn rapidly, some at average speed, some slowly. All have different abilities that they can contribute to the group learning experience if a structure is provided wherein they can do this in the most meaningful and orderly way.

As you begin to prepare, it is important to keep in mind how you relate to your team partner(s). You must work at developing a team identity. This identity will not conflict with but will be in addition to the image you have of yourself as a teacher which we discussed in the preceding chapter. From the outset, look at yourself and your team partner(s) not as two or more individuals but as *one* team. The members of the team are equals; there is no hierarchy. You are simply serving different functions

—but all on the same level. If you are teaching in a team of several members, you may find it desirable to select one who will serve as coordinator, with the job of laying the groundwork, preparing the class for the subject of study, introducing the lesson at the beginning, establishing its goals and the direction of movement which will be taken, and then summarizing the different goals which were accomplished under the leadership of each team member.

The members of the teaching team complement and supplement each other. They all teach on the same day in the same group (unless the large group is divided into task groups with which the teachers may wish to meet individually for a short time). The team approach is *not* an "I teach this week, you teach next week" method, *nor* "I take this part of the group, you take that part," for *neither* of these two approaches is team teaching but only a variation of a one-teacher method of instruction.

Team teaching demands careful preparation by the cooperating teachers. The planning should be done in two ways. First the general scope of the course should be discussed several months in advance at a meeting of all the members of the team. At this time the group should sketch out the direction the course will take for approximately a semester. The first task to accomplish is the establishing of the goals you want to reach. Then in the light of those goals you design the specific elements of the course. You decide in which sessions you will have a speaker or film or which you will devote to a field trip or other special learning experience, and at that time assign responsibilities for procuring such speakers or arranging the details for the special learning experience. The main point to keep in mind, however, is to plan all activities, everything that is said and done, in the light of the goals that have been established first.

The second activity of team planning is the specific session that is held each week among the cooperating teachers in which the main task is to prepare the details of the coming class session. Every week each teacher first prepares individually (reading the lesson materials, meditating, praying), then, following individual preparation, the team members confer at least once either by a meeting or, if the team is composed of only two teachers, by telephone in order to plan how they will approach the upcoming lesson. Each teacher shares in planning how the lesson should be approached, what should be done, what should not be done, who should do what should be done, and how ideas can best be communicated in class.

The class period is divided between the team members, each of whom takes responsibility for a particular area of study. *The process of dividing these responsibilities requires honesty and frankness on the part of the teachers who are cooperating as a team.*

There are at least three criteria that will help in determining the division of labor. You should divide the lesson according to strengths, or *talents*. Let the teacher who draws out discussion well take the responsibility for leading the discussion of the implications of a particular subject under study. Let the teacher who can speak succinctly and in an orderly way do the lecturing that must be done. (When information has to be communicated by this means, let it be done in a maximum of ten minutes at a time and as infrequently as possible.)

You should divide the lesson according to *interests*. Let the teacher who has a particular interest in missions take the responsibility for drawing out the implications of a particular subject for outreach. Let the teacher who has a particular interest in the Bible be responsible for developing the Biblical basis for the study of a particular unit. Let the teacher who has a special interest in the doctrinal aspect of learning develop that part of the lesson.

You should divide the lesson according to *experiences*. Let the teacher who has been to a mission station take responsibility at a particular point in the unit for showing how the subject under discussion is being acted out in that particular area of the world, and how what they are doing there affects us in our mission where we live. Let the teacher who has experienced forgiveness, for instance, in a particularly meaningful way in his or her life, work upon that point in the study of a lesson.

Each teacher should feel free to say: "I have a particular interest in this area. How would it be if I took this part of the lesson this week?" or, "I feel as though I'd like to try working in this area; I've always thought it was an area where I have some strength." Try to develop a relationship where you can be frank with one another, where, if there is a conflict, you can work it through together. Be aware of the other person's strong points also: "Would you like to handle this part, John? You're good at organizing your thoughts and communicating succinctly." The key to the establishing of such a working relationship is love. If you can enter the teaching team with the identity we discussed in Chapter 6, and in love try to develop a small community of reconciliation and companionship within the team itself, you will find that you will have an extremely satisfying experience as a teacher and thus avoid the schism that can cause concern and heartache. Moreover, you will find that you will be teaching more without words concerning the church than you ever will with them.

We have examined the developmental aspects of the

junior high youth, and we have analyzed the main considerations to be dealt with in preparation for meeting the needs of our emerging young adults. But what resources are available for us to use as we seek to employ the principles we have been studying in our teaching situations? This is the subject to which we shall next devote our attention.

PART III

RESOURCES
FOR PRESENTATION

8

Methods
for Communication in Groups

WE HAVE ALREADY LEARNED of the importance that interaction with peers plays in the growth of the adolescent. What, then, are some methods to use in providing learning experiences that are designed to meet the needs of the junior high youth?

The following methods for communicating in groups are techniques that will work with junior highs in general. You may know a number of others, but these methods have been successful with junior highs; more complicated techniques for group interaction have been omitted. You should exercise care at this point, however, for no two groups are exactly the same; what may work well in one group may not be the method to use in another. Some of the following methods may still be a little complex for some of your younger junior highs; you may wish to hold off, for example, with some of the panel-type methods until your students mature more. On the other hand, and only you will be able to tell, some sixth-graders are as mature as many late seventh- and eighth-grade students.

The best way to tell which of the methods to use is to be certain of the goals you the trying to attain. Then determine which of the following methods will best help you accomplish the specific objective that will direct you and your students to the achievement of that goal. Familiarize yourself with all the following methods, come to know your pupils well, and in the light of your goals and the needs and abilities of your junior highs, select the technique that will best serve your purpose. Whatever you do, do *not* simply look through the list to pick out a time filler; this is not education, and both you and your students will quickly perceive this fact and nothing will be gained.

1. *Lecture*

Perhaps the best-known form of teaching is the method of imparting knowledge by which a speaker addresses a group on a given topic. In our age of analysis and questioning of authority, the lecture method of communication has fallen on hard times. Adding to the disrepute of this technique are statistical data such as that considered in our study of learning retention and the awareness of the need to involve pupils in the learning process. However, the lecture method of presentation should not be summarily abandoned because of these reasons; rather, they should provide criteria by which the lecture may be used more effectively than it often has been in the past. It is still a valid and helpful teaching tool when properly used.

The lecture is especially useful in large groups and for the systematic presentation of a specific kind of knowledge to be used as a basis for further discussion. In the classroom, a lecture should never be used apart from some of the following methods of group communication, for such additional activity is necessary to offset the limitations of lecturing: the formality that hinders the exchange of ideas, and the stultifying of growth through the inability of the audience to participate, which results in mind-wandering and discipline problems. However, if the lecture is a carefully prepared oral presentation of a subject by a person qualified in that area, and is accomplished in short periods of time (ten- to fifteen-minute periods at the most) interspersed with pupil participation, the lecture method can be a real help in opening channels of communication that will increase pupil participation.

Student involvement need not come only after the lecture. One very effective method of communicating to a group a certain body of information is to have one of the young people prepare to speak on the subject. This not only provides them with an opportunity to feel that they are accomplishing something important and of value but it involves them in the learning process directly. Moreover, while all young people are highly resistant to indoctrination from outside their youth culture, they are very susceptible to it from within their culture. Hence, while one of their peers is speaking, the other members of the group are more attentive than they would be to an "outsider." The key, however, is preparation, and if you set up a time when you will meet with the person(s) who will be lecturing, you will have no trouble in using this approach.

You may wish to make it easier for youth to be involved in the lecture method of learning by having them team teach together. Ask if two would like to work together, one taking one part of a presentation of a particular subject and the other another part. Such a way of working adds interest not only to those lecturing but also to the audience. Furthermore, learning is increased on both sides of the podium.

There are other methods of communication which are classed in the lecture family. They have valuable alternatives which increase pupil involvement.

a. *Research and Report*

In this method the teacher assigns a topic or topics to be researched and reported on either at the end of the class or at the next class. The whole class is divided into small groups, preferably of three members, who are each assigned a topic of study and are provided with the resource materials with which to secure the needed information. When a report has been prepared through discussion in one of the small groups, its members select from among themselves someone to present their work before the large group.

A variation of this method can be used by simply asking one or two individuals if they will volunteer to do some special study and report their findings to the class as a whole. By having each class member become expert in one area of your study, you will be helping them to meet their identity-forming needs. Each will be standing out in the area in which he has become a resource person. They may give their report at the end of the class, upon returning from the library, or at the beginning of the next class session.

b. *Forum*

The forum method of imparting a body of knowledge has many variations. A simple forum is the giving of information by a resource person using the lecture approach, but there should be an open discussion following the presentation in which the whole audience can participate. There is usually a moderator, which role you as the teacher can best fulfill. The advantages to such a method of teaching are that more opportunity for pupil involvement is possible than under the straight lecture method, and the audience is able to obtain the specific information that it wants on a particular aspect of the subject under discussion. However, this approach is also hindered by the formality that often produces a lack of freedom in which ideas can be interchanged.

Other adaptations of the forum method include a *debate forum,* in which two students present opposing views of an issue, followed by group discussion; the *interview forum,* in which an expert who presents his facts and opinions is questioned by the teacher or, preferably, a student representing the class, followed by discussion involving the whole group; the *lecture forum,* in which group discussion follows a talk by a resource person; the *music forum,* in which the group listens to a musical (instrumental and/or vocal) presentation and then through discussion tries to determine the meaning of that form of expression and how that particular rendition casts light on the subject being studied; the *panel forum,* in which discussion by the group as a whole follows the presentation by a panel; the *sermon forum,* in which a sermon is followed by small-group discussion for a short period, after which the small groups re-form into a large group for further consideration of the topic (perhaps you might ask the pastor to meet with your class in such a context following a sermon that relates directly to a subject you are studying); the *symposium forum,* in which there is discussion of the presentation of a symposium by the entire group; the *film talk-back,* in which discussion follows a film or filmstrip; the *play-reading talk-back,* in which the class discusses a play read for them by several members of the group, each taking a part.

c. *Panel*

Another member of the lecture family, a cousin to the forum, is the panel method of presentation. This technique belongs to the lecture method because it is basically a presentation of a subject to a passive audience, although there are variations of the panel approach that involve the audience in varying degrees. In this method three to six persons who are either especially qualified by virtue of their vocation or students who have done special study on the topic hold a purposeful discussion under the leadership of a moderator. The strengths of this approach are that differing and competent viewpoints spotlight issues, approaches, and angles that would ordinarily not occur to the members of a group, and it stimulates thinking. Followed by methods of group discussion that involve all the pupils, the panel approach is excellent.

As with the forum, there are many variations of the panel method of communication. The following are those which are usable with the average junior high class.

(1) *Expanding Panel*

More commonly known as "fishbowling," the format for this presentation is a circle within a larger circle. A combination presentation and discussion by a panel is followed by the panel's moving back into the larger circle after it concludes its discussion, at a time to be decided by the moderator. When the panel moves back into the circle which expands to make room for them, the entire group discusses the subject in the light of the panel's contribution.

The strengths of this method are that it secures active participation from the whole large group in the second phase of the procedure, and it stimulates interest in a fairly large group. Care should be taken, however, that a number of small discussions do not break out during the second phase. Such a situation could be averted by having the panel members split up instead of joining the large group all in the same place, when entering the expanded circle.

(2) Screening Panel

This technique is undertaken when three to five persons from the audience discuss the needs of the group as a whole with a resource person so that the latter can adjust his presentation to their need on the spot. There may be more than one resource person. The moderator, as usual, may be you, unless you have a particularly mature student, in which case it would be good to have the student be moderator and thus provide a direct learning experience for him and create interest in the audience. The main caution which should be exercised when using this method is that with it you are assuming that the expert is prepared to handle an unexpected need immediately with no further preparation, a premise that should lead you to select your resource person with discrimination.

Similar to the screening panel is the method of the *screened speech*. In this approach, the large group is subdivided into small groups that determine specific areas of concern. These areas of concern are presented to the speaker as questions to which he addresses himself in a speech.

(3) Reaction Panel

A reaction panel is akin to a screening panel, except that the panel of persons from the audience relate to the speaker after rather than before his presentation. The panel (which may also be composed of special resource persons brought in from outside the class) listens to the speaker and then holds a purposeful discussion in reaction to the presentation. This method stimulates the interest of the audience and is successful in clarifying and evaluating an authoritarian point of view. Its main weakness is that it does not allow for the total participation of the whole group present. It can be improved by following it with the forum, as is often done.

(4) *Audience Reaction Team*

The audience reaction team is a type of combination between the screening panel and the reaction panel. Three to five representatives, who may interrupt the speaker at appropriate times for clarification or to help the speaker treat the needs of those present, form a panel from the audience. It is important that this panel be composed of representatives from the audience; this ensures that an audience will understand a difficult subject and it provides stimulation for the large group.

(5) *Interview*

This method is a five- to twenty-minute presentation in which an interviewer (yourself or a mature student) questions and explores aspects of a topic with two or three resource persons who have been given the questions ahead of time. This method is useful in that it draws knowledge from a number of sources to bring light on an issue. Its basic limitation is that it can become disorganized without careful planning of the material to be covered, and it doesn't provide for the participation of all pupils. Open discussion in this case as in all others where such interaction is not provided for within the nature of the method should follow.

(6) *Symposium*

In this approach a panel of persons deliver a speech on as many subjects as there are dimensions of a topic to be considered. The main difference between this approach and the basic panel method which provides its broad characteristics is that a simple panel presentation is an informal discussion on a fairly limited topic. The strengths of this technique are that differing and competent points of view focus on issues, and it stimulates interest and thinking. The limitations are those of the panel method in general.

2. *Group Discussion*

The preceding methods of communication have been primarily presentation-orientated, bringing in pupil involvement principally at the conclusion of the presentation. There are methods of communication, however, which are student-oriented and are designed to help him discover the truth of the realities he is studying. Such methods can be grouped under the broad heading "group discussion," because they all involve the pupil's verbalizing at some place in the learning process (varying at different points according to the method being employed) what he believes about what he is focusing on. Such methods aim at drawing out discussion of all students so that they can grow from the experience of putting into words the concepts they are learning, thereby helping to integrate these concepts into their own identity and life situations.

Group discussion should be the basic framework in which you conduct your teaching. Sit in a large circle, rather than in rows which encourage a lecture-type method of communication and a minimum of pupil response. The circle format in itself teaches nonverbally that each student is important and valued for what he has to contribute, indeed, that he *does* have a contribution to make! The theological premise supporting such a context for teaching is that the Spirit of God is working through all of us, using all of us for the increased edification and upbuilding of everyone. By shutting off or at least not providing for the maximum participation of all pupils, a teacher is limiting the resources or tools the Holy Spirit has available for our instruction and growth.

With this stress on the importance of student participation, whether verbal or nonverbal, there is no implication that this means less work for either you or the students in your class. In your preparation you must determine what goal you are trying to accomplish through discussion, then as you focus on specific objectives to reach the goal(s), you will be able to select the particular form of group discussion out of the ones listed below which are designed to achieve those ends.

In general, there are basically four outcomes that can be reached through group discussion. First, such a method provides the development of understanding and ability in verbal communication, two vital elements in learning to share one's faith. Second, discussion furnishes the opportunity for the student to develop particular skills, attitudes, and personality characteristics, all of which are fundamental in effecting the behavior change essential for growth in Christian maturity and sensitivity for meeting human need. Third, this technique is valuable for the communication of knowledge, an essential element in the establishment of a faith that can be shared. Fourth, discussion supplies the opportunity wherein a pupil may discover knowledge that will enable him to utilize better such information for his own and others' growth.

It is important to keep in mind that discussion is more than conversation. This means that your students are also going to have to prepare before they can engage in significant discussion, otherwise the group experience simply degenerates into a meaningless "pooling of ignorance." The group has to develop a common ground on which to meet in discussing a particular subject.

There are several ways this common ground can be formulated. In the first place, such prior preparation for discussion can be accomplished through homework. However, you may find that your students simply will not read a lesson in a textbook before coming to class. They will give a variety of reasons why they cannot do this: too busy with schoolwork, pressure from home to spend time doing other things, and extracurricular school activities, to name but a few. Now, many of these time-taking involvements of your students are valid. But youth will readily admit, as they have to this writer, that they have time for the things they *want* to do. Furthermore, parents who do not only allow their children to neglect their Christian nurture but also encourage them to become more involved in other activities either directly by pressuring them to obtain certain grades in their schoolwork for example, or indirectly by not showing through word, deed, and attitude the importance of Christian education, are teaching a set of values that is Biblically substandard and they are being remiss in their responsibility. Therefore, if you want your young people to do homework, you should speak to their parents as well as to them. Point out that they as parents can help you accomplish more in class by seeing to it that their children make their church work at least as important as their schoolwork. If this is not communicated, the youth will grow up valuing his faith as less important and relevant than the other dimensions of his life when, indeed, the opposite is true. In secular education the student receives tools to use for an average of seventy years, but in Christian education he is being equipped for eternity!

There is a second method of forming the common ground of preparation necessary for a meaningful class discussion, and you may have to use it, realistically speaking, for parents today are slow to sense and act upon their responsibility to see that their children come to church school prepared. You can set aside the first ten minutes of class time as a study hall in which the class members will read their lesson in the textbook. It would be good to have extra copies of the text handy for those who forget their books and leave them at home. Ask those who have read the lesson either to review or start reading the next lesson. They should receive at least a verbal reward for having completed the assignment, or else the motivation for continuing to do so will be reduced.

A third approach is to use any of the lecture-type techniques of communication in which a body of information would be presented to all at once, thus forming a springboard from which to jump into discussion. The class thus can develop specific points further and then deal with implications for their daily lives from what has been presented.

After you have determined from your general goals what your specific objectives for a given class period will be and that from your general goals you feel a method of group discussion will help you attain your objective(s), you are ready to select which form of group discussion will best help you and your class to accomplish what you desire. The following different types of group discussion have been divided into two parts: (*a*) those in which the entire group functions as a whole, and (*b*) those in which the group as a whole has been subdivided into different parts for the accomplishment of specific functions which will more effectively enable the group as a whole to achieve the objective toward which it is working. By familiarizing yourself with the nature of each method, you will best be able to select the one that is especially designed to accomplish the end you have in mind.

a. *Methods Involving the Group as a Whole*

(1) *Brainstorming (Idea Inventory)*

A good way to begin to solve a problem or to approach a task involving the reaching of a decision is to list first all the possible alternatives that could be employed as answers. From there on the group could discuss the pros and cons of each alternative to determine the best answer. But before evaluation must come a simple listing of the alternatives, and a good method for accomplishing this task is the spontaneous outpouring of ideas for from five to ten minutes. As the group members share their ideas, they are recorded on a chalkboard or overhead projector and are not discussed at this time; quantity at this point is more desired than quality. After a sizable number of alternatives has been listed, the group as a whole or a subcommittee evaluates the merit of each suggestion obtained through brainstorming and thus narrows the list down until the best solution is found. The leader of the group will have to be especially careful in using this method so that discussion of suggestions does not occur until the proper time.

(2) *Case Study*

A real-life situation is presented to the group (without naming the personality involved). The group then discusses the situation in all of its aspects, including alternative solutions or activities, in the attempt to provide a framework for dealing with similar or related situations should any of the members of the group encounter them. This method is especially helpful in developing the ability to share one's faith meaningfully as well as to learn to meet human needs from a Biblical perspective.

(3) *Circular Response* (*Caucus*)

In this method the leader asks each member of a group in turn to state his opinion in regard to a presentation, question, or thought. No one in the group is allowed a second turn to speak until all have spoken once. This is a simple method to draw out the ideas and reactions of all persons in the group, but you are going to have to exercise great caution with its use. It puts a person on the spot, and in so doing may cause someone with a weak ego or a naturally shy person to withdraw and thus hinder his growth instead of developing it. Use this approach carefully, only after you have become well acquainted with all the members of your class, after they have come to know well and trust each other, and after each has grown sufficiently mature to use it.

(4) *Depth Bible Encounter*

This method may be used with either the large group as a whole or the small group. Each member of the class paraphrases a Bible verse or passage in his own words on paper. Then he reads it to either the large group as a whole or to a smaller work group of which he is a member, and they probe him as to its meaning. After the questioning, each person answers verbally or in written form what the implications of that text are for him in his life situation. If this answering is done in written form, the results are then shared with the rest of the members of the group.

(5) *Gallery Conversations*

The climate of an art gallery is established by setting up one or more works of art, whatever form, and the class responds by analyzing the meaning of the message each art form is expressing. Discussion is open and free. If the group as a whole is in excess of eight to ten persons, it would be good to subdivide into smaller groups, with each small group analyzing a different work of art and then presenting its conclusions to the whole group through a reporter who has been recording the observations of his small group.

(6) *Question and Answer*

One of the oldest methods of teaching involving pupil response is the question-and-answer technique. It is a method that Jesus used frequently. And the accounts of Jesus' use of question and answer should be read carefully, for there is an art in the use of this method of teaching, and Jesus employed it well.

There are several principles that must be employed for the most effective use of questions in teaching. We can here identify at least nine.

(a) *Use questions that facilitate transfer.*

Ask questions such as: "How do you feel about that, Tom? Why?" "Do you agree with what Tom said, Mary? Why or why not?" "What must have been going through Gideon's mind when God told him to send almost all his troops home, Sam?" "What would you have done if you were Paul in this case, Bill?" "How would you have felt if you were Mary, Joan?" "How would you explain this to a non-Christian, anybody? Ron?" "What did John just say, Pete? Tell us in your own words." "Do you agree; do you see it that way? Why?" "You haven't said much, Jill. What do you think?" "How would you evaluate that comment, Phil?" "Why did God lead the Israelites to Canaan, Jan?" "What other areas of your life does this truth we've been discussing have meaning for, Don?" "What is meant by the term 'Trinity,' Jim? Explain that for us. What does it mean to you?"

(b) *Ask questions that require an explanation.*

Stay away from questions that can be answered by a "Yes" or a "No" whenever possible. Otherwise, that may be all you'll get as a response. If you do ask a "Yes" or "No" question (they're not all bad), follow it up with a "Why" or "Why not?" Then ask another person in the group if he agrees.

(c) *Draw out shy students.*

Take particular care to bring shy students into the discussion. It is very important that they learn to express themselves so that they, too, can develop the ability to communicate their faith. This will be one of your greatest challenges in teaching; it will also be one of the best opportunities you have for Christian ministry. It will be difficult, but don't give up. Ask easier (though not simpleminded) questions. Ask, for example, questions where there is no clearly right or wrong answer in order to build their self-confidence. Reward verbally those answers which are good and the answers which have come from shy people. Don't make it fake or obvious. A simple "Good point" or "All right, real good" following an answer from a shy person that was offered with a great deal of difficulty will enable that person to grow greatly in the course of the year—and you will have accomplished a great ministry in the Kingdom of God.

(d) *Let a pause develop.*

If a question you have asked isn't answered immediately after you have asked it, give the group a few moments in which to think more deeply. If you ask Tom a question and he just sits there, don't panic; simply say in a relaxed manner, "All right, take a minute to think." This statement puts the group (and especially yourself) at ease, and it makes Tom feel important in his own eyes —you didn't quickly jump to someone else, but you counted him significant enough to want to hear his answer, and since he realizes this, he will more than likely answer you as best he can. This won't work 100 percent of the time, but it usually will. If he doesn't answer, it is no aspersion against you or your teaching, nor will it be perceived as such by the group or anyone else, so calmly say something along the line of, "All right, Tom, you keep thinking and, meantime, how would you answer that question, Joe?" As far as the length of the pause is concerned, don't be afraid to let it become at least fifteen to twenty seconds or more. It may seem like an eternity to you at first, but you will soon become confident in handling such situations and both you and the group will develop confidence in group discussion. After all, this is one of the most important aspects of your job, to develop with the group the ability and confidence to express your faith meaningfully. Through this and other forms of discussion, you will be ministering to the identity-forming adolescent by allowing him to grow in his own self-understanding as he hears his faith voiced and takes note of how it is received by others.

(e) *Ask the question first, then call on someone.*

Don't call on a person and then state the question, for this will draw the attention only of the person called on plus those others who happen to be listening. Instead, state the question and then call on someone; in this way everyone listens to the question in case he will be called on. Thus you maintain control of the group better and retain their attention easier.

(f) *If you are team teaching, sit apart from your partner(s).*

Don't sit beside your partner if you are teaching as a team. You then appear as a panel, and it is easier to fall into the lecture method of communication than if you sit apart. If team teaching, the most effective position to assume is directly across from a partner. This position also aids in minimizing discipline problems, for a teacher is never far from any one student in the group, and the number of students sitting right next to a teacher is doubled.

(g) *Sit with the students as much as possible.*

Don't stand. All teachers in the group-discussion method of teaching should sit in the circle format with the students. The basic assumption behind group discussion as a method of teaching is that learning can occur through the mutual sharing of thoughts on a particular topic, that all members of the group have something important to contribute. If one or two in the group (teachers) stand when the rest of the group is sitting, this says (nonverbally) that what they have to say is more important than what anyone else will say. It is also very easy to revert to lecturing when the teachers stand. It should be remembered that at times the lecture method of communication is good to use, and it can be used within a group discussion context; in fact, lecturing should always be done within this context. However, the above comments are intended only as a caution so that when the intent is to discuss as a group you won't fall back into a method of communication you didn't intend to use, thereby jeopardizing your objective.

(h) *Be careful of diversions.*

Don't let discussion get sidetracked. Diversions are important sometimes, but not all the time. However, don't feel bad if the discussion gets sidetracked and you spend the rest of the period on the diversion *if* you sense that it is meeting a real need of the students and is something that they are very seriously concerned to know about. Do, however, curtail the diversion if it is not important to their Christian growth.

(i) *Before you tell them, ask them.*

Don't hand them everything on a silver spoon. The greatest and most meaningful learning comes when the student discovers for himself a truth you are trying to teach. This is also how you maintain his interest. A good rule of thumb is never tell a student anything you can get him to tell you. For example, don't say, "Today we are studying about Moses, who led the people of Israel out of the land of Egypt through the Sinai desert up into the Land of Canaan." Rather say, "Whom are we studying about?" "Who were the people he was a part of, Tom?" "What did Moses do with these people, Sue?" "Where did they go?" "How did they get there?" "What did they think about while all this was happening?" "How would you have felt?" These are just a few examples of how you

can use the method of asking questions to lead students
to the discovery of the truth you are intending to teach.

(7) *Role-Playing*

An especially helpful method of communication which
will aid you in reaching the second main goal of Christian
education, that of developing sensitivity to the needs of
others and ability to meet those needs, is the role-play. In
this technique, members of the class cast themselves as
actors do in the various parts of a given situation, identifying with the persons in that situation so much that what
they say and do is no longer themselves but the person
they are portraying; for a moment they become the person whose identity they are assuming. In so doing, they
grow in their own identity formation as they are presented
with the opportunity to distinguish between themselves
and the personality they are portraying. They come to be
able to say, "This I am, but this is not me."

The acting out of the situation in role-playing is done
without rehearsal and is limited to only a few minutes in
duration, stopping at a high point for discussion of what
happened and how what happened sheds light on what
you want them to learn. This spontaneous action out of
a situation by persons you select emphasizes relationships
and attitudes which are then discussed by all.

There are at least four contributions that role-playing
makes to your classroom teaching. First of all, it provides
for transfer of learning through dealing with specific problems in such a way that students can see a verbal message
come to life as it hits them where they live. Secondly, it
stimulates pupil participation, especially in the form of
discussion when used at the beginning of a session.
Thirdly, it is helpful in enabling the students to gain in-

sight into why other people think and act the way they do, thus aiding them in developing an approach that will equip them to minister in such situations. Fourthly, role-play helps one to develop skill in ministering in simulated situations where learning can occur through mistakes that harm no one, so that such mistakes can be avoided when they are encountered in actual situations.

Learning is facilitated when concepts can be seen applicable to a situation. Hence, role-play has a great value in the Christian education classroom. It not only enables the student to visualize the situation but also gives him the opportunity to learn how to react in such a situation so that he can make the best Christian response to similar circumstances in life.

The key to role-play is to give the group a good situation with fairly specific details. At the same time, tell the people involved in the role-play exactly what you want them to do. This guidance will enable them to reach the objectives you want them to attain through this method of group discussion. (Such specific situations have already been provided under the trade name Squirms by the Contemporary Drama Service, Downers Grove, Illinois.)

(8) Educational Games

(a) Exercises

There are a number of instructional "games" which involve the group in different activities designed to enable the participants to discover what you want to learn. Some of these exercises are written, an example of which is to be found in Appendix B, and others are acted out in different forms of interpersonal encounter.

An example of the latter is "Giving and Receiving," where six to eight people, standing in a circle, are told to give the leader something when he walks around the circle and taps them on the shoulder. Unknown to anyone in the group, however, the leader intends to use only two of the members in the exercise. He taps one member on the shoulder, and after receiving something from that person walks around and gives it to another. Upon walking around the circle again, making it look as though he might tap someone else, he taps the first man again. Upon receiving something, he gives it to the same one who received the first object he gave. The leader repeats this process several times and then instructs the group to return to their seats. At this point the leader discusses what happened, how the two felt, how the others who were rejected felt, and where in our lives similar occurrences take place, how we feel about them, and what resources we have available to help us deal with such happenings. Such a game teaches many concepts, but the main use it has for this age group is the vivid lesson each person experiences concerning personal acceptance in the Christian life.

There are many such exercises available, and junior high youth respond to them with much enthusiasm. (One fine way to learn them, and, moreover, to grow in your own self-understanding is to enroll in a Christian sensitivity training course.) You can even encourage your students to create a game themselves. Other sources are the handbooks of *Structural Experiences for Human Relations Training,* by J. William Pfeiffer and John E. Jones. In using exercises that may elicit deep feelings be cautious, for not all exercises should be used in a regular classroom situation, and some should be used only by leaders with training in group dynamics.

In addition to being very helpful in creating motivation

to learn, games promote discussion, provide learning in decision-making which goes deeper than simple multiple choice, create an awareness of other persons' needs and desires, enable the learner to experience different realities and the effect on them of various Christian solutions, build relationships, develop new behavioral responses, reinforce a unit of study on the subject the game deals with as any visual aid or creative expression aid would do, stimulate self-expression, and induce hard thinking. Games are also useful in teaching factual information, though some researchers are unwilling to conclude that using games facilitates the learning of facts any more than other methods of teaching do, and they are inclined to stress the uses of this technique mentioned above as having more positive value for the classroom. However, you will find, as has this writer, that these exercises are helpful also in regard to factual knowledge *if* they are supplemented with other methods such as work sheets and group discussion, the latter of which should follow all games.

(b) *Simulation*

Another type of educational game is called simulation, and it attempts to do just what its name suggests. The game re-creates a life situation in a laboratory setting in such a way that the players experience directly a number of the constructive and destructive forces at work in the actual situation that is being modeled. Simulation games appear in three different forms: those which involve working within a system, those which focus on interpersonal relationships, and those which function in a combination of the first two. The uses of simulation games parallel those identified above, and are especially helpful for leading the learner into an understanding of the framework within which human interaction takes place, what the forces are and the causes that are operating therein, and what the youth can do about this situation, especially if he finds himself involved in a similar circumstance in his own life. You can obtain further information on simulation games from The Center for Simulation Studies in St. Louis.

b. *Methods Involving Subgroups*

(1) *Buzz or Work Groups*

Especially when the group as a whole is large—consisting of more than ten persons including the teacher(s)—you may find it wise to spend considerable time in smaller subgroups in which much of the work is accomplished and then reported back to the group as a whole through recorders representing each subgroup. It is good when using this method for the teacher to assign the recorder in each group, for this enables them to begin to work more quickly at their task without becoming entangled in a web of group dynamics involving leadership. Also, be sure to have a pencil and paper ready for each recorder, then simply hand it to the person you select. Much anxiety is usually relieved at that point, and the person who has the task of jotting down the observations of the group (in addition to his contributing as a regular member) clearly spelled out to him does not have to worry about how his peers will evaluate his different relationship to them. Don't laugh! Even so small a circumstance could be catastrophic to an identity-forming youth with a weak ego, who is so dependent on what his peers are thinking that he doesn't want to be different from them. Especially if they sense his dependence on them, the peers can be ruthlessly cruel in their treatment of behavior that they regard as deviant from what they determine is the norm of the youth culture, thus threatening their own identity. Yet you need not fear for the one you select if you casually request him to be the recorder for his group, handing him a pencil and a piece of paper at the same time. He will understand that even when he reports to the whole group, it is not his views that he is expressing (even though he identifies with most of them), but those of his group (strength in numbers). At the same time, he is receiving education in learning to express himself.

Make your subgroups of from three to five members each. Divide them by sex for the most part, especially for the first several times that you use this method. Junior high young people are more inclined to open up if with members of their own sex in the small groups. They are too much concerned with how what they say as an individual is received by a member of the opposite sex to communicate freely. Yet, that kind of dialogue is precisely what we want in buzz groups. There is also the positive fact that girls will approach certain subjects with a point of view entirely different from that of boys. When they are in small groups by themselves, they will bring out the different perspectives which can then be reported through the recorder without individual fear.

Two additional principles of good buzz grouping are imperative for the success of this method in contributing to your goals and objectives. First be sure to *define* the task of each group *clearly*. Write the task you want the groups to achieve either on the chalkboard or on the overhead projector, and leave it there throughout the duration of their work so that they can refer to it when needed. This will help them to stay on the subject and accomplish the objective you have for them. As a general rule, have each subgroup work at the same task; this will enable the group as a whole to receive a wider variety of viewpoints and insights. However, as some of the small-group activities below indicate, there are advantages in having subgroups work at different tasks occasionally.

Second, *always, always* re-form into the large group as a whole to combine insights from each task group. Have each recorder read one comment at a time form his group. Let the recorder from Subgroup A read the first of his comments, then the recorder from Subgroup B read the first of his, and so on. Don't allow each recorder to read all the comments his group came up with, because rapid movement with a number of different people speaking alternately keeps up interest and alertness. And in this way the last subgroup to report will not have all its "thunder" stolen by the time it gets to report, thereby feeling as though the work that it went through was useless, with a resultant lack of desire to repeat the process on another occasion. Be sure to allow sufficient time for each subgroup to report. It is good to keep things moving in order to keep up interest. Don't allow more than ten to fifteen minutes in a subgroup on the average, and be sure to allow for reporting at the end of each task.

(2) *Couple Buzzers*

This method is a variation of the slightly larger buzz group technique and is characterized by the division of the whole group into couples for a brief period during which they discuss a particular subject that has been assigned. For example, "For the next ten minutes you are to discuss places you visit daily where you could be especially on the lookout for opportunities to share your faith, and list *at least* ten such places on the sheet of paper which I will now give you." Be sure in assigning a task such as the one above that you say "at least" before the number, for some especially sharp students may attain that number very soon after you start, long before the others, and you could wind up with a discipline problem on your hands.

As with the regular buzz groups, noise will be no problem, since people engaged in meaningful conversation are oblivious to other couples or groups even a shoulder's length away. Also, as with the buzz-group method and other group-discussion techniques as well, you must keep the activities moving. Don't plan to spend half of the class time with any one method; even adults don't like to remain at the same task indefinitely. Besides, when there is a definite time limit, students are more likely to get down to business than if they think they have the whole period. As with *all* other methods of working with subgroups, have the parts report back to the whole at the completion of the task through a predesignated recorder.

(3) *Reality-Practice*

The name of this method is especially fitting, for it presents an opportunity for you to accomplish exactly what you are trying to do in Christian education, namely, to provide a laboratory experience in which your students can develop the ability to share their faith and to meet human needs as they encounter them. It is also another valuable aid in helping the student to develop further his self-concept, as he sees himself growing in the ability to deal with many different situations and how others (especially the objective observer) react to him in these situations.

This method of communication in groups is a combination of role-play and buzz grouping. The group is divided into subgroups of three, and a situation is read to all groups. For example, "You are in the cafeteria at school during lunch period and you notice that the friend sitting next to you looks very sad and dejected. When you ask him what the matter is, he replies that he just doesn't find any meaning in life and he wonders why he should live at all. He feels his parents love his older brother and younger sister more than they do him; in fact, he feels they really hate him. Your friend is a non-Christian. In the light of what we've been studying, what is your response to him?"

Each member of each subgroup plays each of three roles. One person is himself, a Christian, another is the person with the problem, and the third member of the subgroup is an observer. All the subgroups work on the same situation. After three minutes of role-playing stop the conversations. Then have the observer in each group share his observations with the two role-players along two lines: first, what the Christian said that was good, meaningful, persuasive; and second, what he didn't say that he could have. Let the observer speak for not longer than two minutes, then have everyone in the subgroup exchange roles and role-play the same situation following the same format; then do it all a third time so that everyone has an opportunity at each role. Following the completion of this method, hold an open discussion concerning what the group thinks were the best responses. List these responses on the chalkboard or the overhead projector as they are offered by the group. Then ask for two volunteers to role-play the same situation in front of the whole group. Another variation of this method is the use at the end, during the role-play by volunteers, of a panel of judges not of the class, who would evaluate everyone's performance (all would role-play by twos at the end), the best to receive some reward. The key to role-play is to have a realistic situation with fairly specific details.

(4) Demonstration—Work Group

A person or small group shows the whole group how to perform a certain function. Following this demonstration, the whole group is subdivided into small groups where everyone has the opportunity to work at developing the skills learned through the presentation. Volunteers could then perform the function in front of the group when the small groups re-form. This method could be combined with reality-practice in which one small group that has had prior instruction, such as three of your best students from last year's class, role-plays a situation first, after which it goes to the whole group as described above.

(5) Group Drawing or Writing

These are two separate group exercises. The only difference is what is being done; the basic format remains the same. The group is subdivided into small groups which are given a specific task to accomplish: for example, to discuss the meaning of a particular passage of the Bible for five minutes. At the end of five minutes, the groups are given the following task: "Now, in the light of what you have discussed, express your conclusions in the form of a drawing [or poem, or story, or responsive reading]—one drawing [or poem, etc.] from each group." Give the subgroups only fifteen to twenty minutes (specify which and *keep to it*) to complete their project. Then have one subgroup at a time display their drawing or read to the group their literary work, and let the group respond freely, interpreting what they see or hear. Next, have the subgroup whose work has been interpreted respond with reactions to the interpretations of the whole group, agreeing or disagreeing (and why) and adding anything to the interpretation that was omitted or not observed by the large group. Repeat the process for each subgroup.

(6) Inductive Bible Study

It is important when studying the Bible not to take passages or verses out of context. The method of inductive Bible study helps to teach the importance of knowing the context of a given passage, as well as to provide the pupil participation which creates not only interest in learning what the Bible teaches but also the best learning in terms of greatest retention and transference.

In this method, the five W's of journalism plus How? are applied to a particular passage of the Bible. The group is divided into subgroups, each of which approaches the text with a different question. One subgroup wrestles with the question of *who* wrote the passage and *who* received it. Another buzz group tries to answer *what* the author is writing about. Another subgroup has the question of *where* the author wrote and *where* the story took place. A fourth group (or, if there are less than four subgroups, a second question for the first group) has the task of finding *when* the text was written. A fifth question to be dealt with is *why* the author wrote what he did, and sixth, *how* he is saying it.

The buzz, or work, groups (same type of group; both names are often used interchangeably, and frequently the term "task group" is also used, meaning the same thing) are given commentaries, Bible dictionaries, and any other tools they may need, and are assigned a specific amount of time in which to complete their task, following which they report back to the whole group the findings they have made. Following the subgroup reports, the whole group discusses the question, In the light of all these facts (who, what, where, etc.), what does this passage mean in terms of what I believe and do in my life? (Different subgroups may be formed for this discussion.)

(7) Reaction or Listening Teams

This method is used, as the name suggests, with a teaching technique of the lecture type. Subgroups are asked to listen with a specific question in mind. Such questions could be adapted from the five W's and How? Following the speaker or film, each subgroup spends a maximum of ten minutes gathering its individual input into a group response. The subgroups then report to the whole group the results of their corporate efforts, and the group tries to ascertain the meaning of the presentation for the Christian life.

3. Project

Another method of communicating the truth of a lesson is by having the pupils in a group participate in a project. For example, in a unit of study in which you are trying to teach the fact that the deepest fulfillment and satisfaction in life is through caring for someone else out of a response to God's care for us through Christ, you could help your students discover this truth for themselves by suggesting that they develop a project such as making baskets of foodstuffs for needy people at Thanksgiving or through a class calling program at a neighborhood rest home for the aged. Through discussion in which the group compares its feelings following the service project with its feelings following the meeting of personal needs, you will have created the context for the students to discover the connection between service and satisfaction.

Careful preparation of the project is essential. As with other teaching methods, it has to be designed to meet one of your objectives. Another element integral to the success of the project is the involvement of your class in its preparation. You should make suggestions, but let the students be as much involved in the decision-making as in the observation of the truth the project will enable them to discover. Thus they will not only be learning while setting up the project but also be motivated to follow through with it, since it is largely their idea and creation. They have a vested interest in it.

4. *Field Trip*

A method of communication which highly stimulates learning and which provides for total pupil involvement in the learning process is the field trip, a class excursion to a place that provides the opportunity for students to observe firsthand the skills or knowledge that you want them to have. This method must never be used by itself, however, but should always be followed by group discussion. For example, in learning the mission of the church, you might find it helpful at one point in your study to take a field trip to one of the city missions near you. Before going you could assign different tasks to different subgroups: one group could look specifically for what methods are used at the mission for outreach; another group could be responsible for finding out the history of the mission, what its original purposes were and if they are still being followed today, and if not, why not; another group could be asked to identify the ways in which the gospel message is related to the social needs of the people the mission serves. Upon returning from the field trip, the members of the various subgroups could meet together to plan the presentation of their findings to the whole group. They should conclude by discussing the implications of what they have learned for their life situations.

In this method of communication much learning takes place. However, it should be planned well, and if you are teaching alone, it would be good for you to ask some other adults to help you chaperone. As for such details as publicity, refreshments, transportation, let the young people have responsibility for these tasks; it will help them to develop the leadership qualities that are within them. But they will need your oversight and encouragement, and it would be well to let their parents know what responsibility they have, to be sure that the job gets done. *Make sure* that you tell the parents not to do this job themselves. Ask them to check occasionally with their youngster to see that he is doing it. This also helps the parents to become interested in what their son or daughter is doing in church school.

This has been an examination of the methods of group interaction which can be used well with junior high youth. There are many other resources available to you in the form of audio-visual aids. An examination of these will provide the subject for our next chapter.

9
Audio and Visual Aids

WE HAVE DISCOVERED that a learner retains 10 percent of what he hears only, 65 percent of what he observes through seeing and hearing combined, 80 percent of what he says, and 90 percent of what he does. The last two figures, indicating the importance of pupil involvement, imply that the student should be active in the learning process. Methods for providing such activity have been examined in the preceding chapter. In our present discussion we will seek to discover the implications of the first two figures for our classroom teaching situations.

Paul Vieth has produced the results of studies that further substantiate the increase of learning when audio-visual aids are employed in teaching. Through a comparison of three groups studying the life of Paul—a control group using no audio-visual aids, another group using a series of sound motion pictures, *The Life of St. Paul,* and a third group using a set of filmstrips compiled from certain frames of the motion pictures—it was found that, all other factors being equal, the group that used the filmstrips learned 24.51 percent more than the group that used no extra aids, and the group using the motion pictures learned 38.52 percent more than the group without aids. The filmstrip group learned less than the one with the sound motion pictures, but considerably more than the control group.[26]

As we thus see, it is generally assumed among educators that there is no doubt that the use of audio-visual materials greatly increases learning. However, the use of such resources is principally a simple variation of the lecture method of communication. Would combining such a presentation with pupil participatory activities such as those we considered in the last chapter increase the learning potential? The answer is a resounding "Yes!"

A study at Yale University was made with four different groups, one that simply saw a film, a second that was given a set of questions on the film before they viewed it, a third that was given a set of participatory exercises at the end of each of the seven sections of the film, and a fourth that combined what the second and third groups had in addition to the film. The results of controlled experimentation under these conditions produced the following statistics showing the gain in learning of each group: the first group, 8.2 percent; the second, 10.5 percent; the third, 12.2 percent; and the fourth, 14 percent.[27]

Hence, in your teaching always use a film or filmstrip or any of the following audio-visual aids for what it is, an *aid* to help in illustrating a point in a lesson and not as a lesson in itself. Never show a film, for example, without at least discussing it and relating it to the point you have already made which it is illustrating.

These aids are designed to facilitate retention. As we have seen in our discussion of human learning, transfer is not only an integral dimension of the general learning process but is fundamental to Christian education. Thus pupil involvement with an audio-visual aid is essential. Audio-visuals should not become crutches upon which we put our whole weight.

As with all instructional materials, audio-visuals should be used only as they further the attainment of a specific objective. They are used to help develop a point already made or to introduce a point to be expanded further, but never be a point in themselves.

One general observation concerning audio-visual aids is that the teacher must be very careful in selecting which aids he will use in his class situation. Some filmstrips, for example, are designed for use only with preschool and primary children, others deal specifically with adult concerns, and it is just as disastrous to use materials which are too much beneath the level of your young people as to operate over their heads. In both such cases you are communicating the idea that Christian education, the church, and God are irrelevant to their lives.

Having briefly considered the place and functions of audio-visual aids, we shall now look specifically at the aids themselves and the use they have for you as you teach junior highs. For our purposes here, we shall divide them into three areas, using as a line of demarcation their technical composition, that is, whether they are principally audio, visual, or audio-visual aids. However, it should be noted that even a flat picture, while principally only a visual aid, is in a very real way an audio-visual aid, for when properly used it is employed with discussion—hence the audio aspect of its contribution. Similarly, devices that are primarily audio in nature, such as the record player, may be used with written exercises which provide a visual dimension to reinforce what is heard. There are an unlimited number of possibilities which can be employed through combination of the following resources, especially when they are utilized with the methods of group communication which have been considered in the preceding chapter and also when they are used with such creative self-expression aids as will be discussed in the following chapter. If you want to be a creative teacher who will be able to stimulate your students to greater learning, you can do so through combinations like these— and through prayer.

1. Audio Aids

a. Record Player

One of the best-known and most often used audio aids is the record player, and it is an excellent teaching aid for the junior high age group. As anyone who has any awareness of what is going on in the world knows, teen-agers are high on records. Fortunately, Christian education leaders and publishers have produced a number of excellent recordings on a variety of subjects, and there is coming to be an increasing quantity of such productions on the market today.

For junior high classes, it is instructive to take a hit recording in the top ten being listened to currently, play it in class and then discuss what it is saying. Much popular music today has a good deal of theological significance. Many of the implications behind what is being sung today both agree and disagree with what we believe as Christians; it is good that your students can distinguish which is which in what they are listening to each day of the week. Through such discussion you can help them transfer what they are learning conceptually into what they are encountering in their daily lives. As they grow in their ability to make this transfer they will be able to express their faith more meaningfully on these subjects in witnessing situations. By being able to relate their faith to the statements made in a song, a student would have a very good springboard for launching a witnessing opportunity by saying something like, "Man, Swish, that's groovy music, but I sure can't cut those words when it says—"

When you use recordings, play all the way through once what you want your class to listen to, then play it in context up to the first point you want them to discuss, stop the record at that place and ask, for example: "What does that statement mean, Jim?" "Do you agree with that, Mary? Why?" "How does this statement in the song relate to what we have just been studying in Ephesians, John? How would you communicate that to the singer of this song?"

b. *Tape Recorder*

In addition to the record player, another popular audio aid that has many uses for the classroom is the tape recorder. This device is excellent for getting discussion started by playing back in class a radio or television program that has bearing on a particular lesson. Be sure to play only that part of the radio or TV program which has relevance to the point you are trying to lead the students to discover; don't replay a large portion of the program, but just enough to give the gist of what has been said. Then ask different individuals to comment on what has been played back.

The recorder is also useful for taping a role-play in class. During the discussion of what was said in the role-play you can replay a particular part of the conversation in order to bring that aspect to attention for discussion.

Typical questions helpful in guiding the discussion at this point include: "What was John trying to say here?" "How did you feel when he said that, Mary?" "What would you have said at that point, Tom? Why?"

You can also tape your own role-play during the week's preparation and apply it to your class for illustration and discussion of a particular point you want to make in a lesson. You can also tape a reading for the students to listen to, and then play again brief parts you want them to discuss in particular.

You can tape a resource person, an expert in a field that has a bearing on a subject your class is studying, and play back his comments at relevant points in the study. Of course this should only be done if the person cannot come in person to your class, which would be the best arrangement, but certainly a tape of him is a desirable second-best.

A less expensive type of tape recorder is now on the market which uses cassettes that slip in and out very easily and quickly. In addition to ease and inexpensiveness, the cassette recorder allows an increased amount of recording time for small machines. Very compact, they are also easy to handle and ideal for the classroom.

c. *Telephone*

Another audio device that can be used with effectiveness with the junior high age group, especially because they use it frequently in their daily lives, is the telephone. The creative teacher can find many ways in which the telephone can be used, and thus aid in homework's being accomplished. One possibility, by way of example, is associated with a unit on prayer. To help convey the meaning and importance of intercessory prayer, you could set up a prayer chain among your class members. You can tell the class to call you whenever anyone is sick, has a long trip coming up, is facing an important test, has to go to the hospital, or would like to feel the care of others and the strength of God. You would then call two others who would in turn call two others until each member of the class was informed of a particular need for which he would then offer prayer. Be sure to place your own needs in the chain occasionally to overcome any hesitancy on the part of the students.

Two items are important in the success of such a technique. First, considerable work is going to have to be accomplished beforehand in establishing a climate of acceptance and concern for each other. This will come partly as the group begins to develop a group consciousness somewhat naturally. But you will also have to help it along quite a bit through building and showing an attitude of love toward each person as he is and communicating the fact that everyone has a need for help at times and that the church exists to provide that help. You will have to teach that help is to be desired, not scorned (such is the negative value that our American culture places on the need for help). Similarly, you will have to undo the stigma that praying for someone is consigning him to hell or helplessness. All too often when someone says, "I'm praying for you," he is being judgmental and cynical. Unfortunately, our junior highs are aware of this by now, but it is not too late for you to help them relearn the proper, Biblical understanding of what it means to pray for someone.

Secondly, you will have to have the prayer chain well planned. Each person will have to be made aware of whom he is to call. It would be good to give each student a list of the whole chain and on it spell out his exact responsibility. From time to time you should remind them of the chain and where they are in it, especially if it hasn't been used a great deal. Do not hesitate in getting the chain started to ask them to pray for you. This will help to create a desire within them to use the device.

You can also put the chain to other uses, such as reminding the class of a homework assignment, adding to or subtracting from an assignment, or reminding the class of the Friday night hayride.

d. Speed Listening

A new method of audio learning called speed listening is being developed in which various machines eliminate unneeded sounds in the human speech to enable the listener to learn more in less time. When this method becomes available for Christian education, care should be exercised to use discussion with it so that it does not become a form of indoctrination against which the youth will rebel.

2. Visual Aids

a. Flat Pictures

Perhaps the best-known and certainly one of the oldest forms of visual aid is the flat picture. You have right in your own home many sources of pictures that can be applied to your classroom situation. It would be a great help if you began a file system of materials which you could catalog according to subject or type of aid. For example, you could file materials you find in newspapers, magazines, posters, calendars, and photographs either under subjects such as "Love," "Church," "Sin," "Salvation," "Service," or under types of aids such as "Flat Pictures,"

"Charts," and the others listed below. From this teacher's experience the former method of classification seems to make materials most readily accessible.

Be sure to involve the pupils in the use of such aids. Do not tell your class what a picture is describing at first. Two very useful ways to use flat pictures are the following: (1) Begin by asking the students to describe what they feel the picture is saying. What is happening in the picture? Who are the people in the picture? Are they happy or sad? Why? (2) Begin by saying, "All right, I'm going to let you look at this picture for thirty seconds— study it carefully." Then at the end of exactly thirty seconds turn the picture around so that only you can see it and have the students tell you what they saw, what the message is that the picture is communicating. Then by discussion lead them to explain the relationship between what the picture is expressing and what they have been learning in the current unit of study.

b. *Charts*

Charts provide another valuable method of teaching for the junior high teacher. As with all other instructional methods, the use of a chart should be determined by the objectives you are trying to have the pupils attain. There are different types of charts, each of which is useful for the accomplishment of different purposes. The presentation of facts alone is well done through the use of an outline chart. Of course, since the junior high student is now capable of functioning intellectually in concepts, such facts ought to be used as a means for developing a concept and not memorized simply for their own sake. Thus, as with the other visual aids, a method of group discussion or creative self-expression should be used with the chart presentation. Comparative information is easily communicated through the use of a tabular chart. A sequence of events is more easily understood when a time-line chart is used. This method also helps to give continuity to a number of lessons which span several weeks' duration. There are other types of charts as well, but their use is limited mostly to teaching younger children.

Christian publishing houses which produce curricula for the church school provide charts that deal with a number of subjects. However, it is instructive and a valuable learning tool if your pupils can themselves develop a chart specifically for use in your class which will pertain to the unit you are studying. Such activity not only provides the pupil involvement which is so vital to retention and transfer as well as motivation, but also aids in reinforcing what is being learned. A variety of materials can be used in making charts: newsprint, shelf-lining paper, book paper (which can be purchased from a paper supply company) or chart and cover paper (which can be obtained from either a paper supply company or an art supplies store).

c. *Bulletin Boards*

Bulletin boards also provide valuable visual aids. On the board, use captions that express exactly what you want to teach regarding a certain unit. Lay out the materials that will be mounted on the board in the order in which the eye naturally follows in reading: from left to right, from up to down. An excellent use of the bulletin board for junior high teaching is to show relationships. For example, the word "Service" could be attached to the upper left corner of the board and a strip of construction paper could extend from the word to a picture of a young teen-ager raking the leaves on the lawn of an elderly lady.

As with charts, it is best if you help the students create their own bulletin board, thereby motivating them to interest in the subject and providing the context for discovery. Flat materials work well, and can be given added effect through making them three-dimensional by attaching paper squares to their backs. Be sure to keep the bulletin board up to date. Do not have Christmas materials still displayed at Easter time, or even in January!

d. *Chalkboard*

Another basic visual aid is the chalkboard, and it is especially helpful, for it has a variety of uses: it can display drawings that will illustrate a point you want to make—even simple stick figures appeal to both children and adults; flat pictures may be displayed on a chalkboard (be sure not to use cellophane tape, which will leave marks); and, of course, it is used most often for all kinds of writing purposes including the introduction of new words, the presentation of a sequence of events, and for teaching songs, making announcements, oral testing, recording the comments of buzz group recorders and other group interaction, as well as listing questions to keep in mind while viewing a film or filmstrip or when listening to a form of lecture. Color chalk adds interest as does having your students take part in writing on the chalkboard. Take care at this point, though, that you don't force a student to write on the board if he does not want to. He may be a poor speller, and the embarrassment of making mistakes might well cause him to withdraw into a shell, just the opposite of what you want for him as you try to help him develop the ability to express what he believes. Feel free to ask your pupils to write; if they say no, fine, let it go. But all won't refuse, and allowing them to use the board whenever possible will create interest not only for the one writing but also for the rest of the class, and it will provide important reinforcement in what is being learned. Whenever these benefits occur, there is a reduction in discipline problems. One last point deserves to be made: always erase your chalkboard when you are finished, for it may contain information that it is well others outside the group do not become aware of (older classes may criticize your youngsters for being concerned about such "childish" problems), and it is an act of courtesy for the next teacher who may use your room.

e. *Maps*

Maps provide another valuable tool for classroom instruction, and there are a variety of them. There are single maps which lie out flat, there are map stands which contain a series of maps in a flip-chart fashion, there are relief maps of Palestine, and the globe is also a valuable map resource. Excellent map stands can be obtained from denominational and other church supply stores. Map stands offer fine comparisons between Old and New Testament Palestine as well as maps showing the great empires of Bible times and how their influence affected the life and faith of the Hebrews and early Christians. Maps are also produced for the overhead projector which have transparent overlays showing, for example, the path that Moses and the Israelites took during their exodus from Egypt to Sinai, and another overlay showing the trip from Sinai to Palestine. As with other visual aids, it is better if the students can make their own to coincide with a particular unit. Even relief maps can be made from flour and salt, clay, or plaster of paris.

f. *Classroom Walls*

Do not fail to use the very classroom walls as teaching devices. Display on them the work your students do, especially their individual as well as their group work. However, when using the walls for this purpose, be sure you don't display only the work of a few selected students who do exceptionally well. Pick the best work of the students who do the least attractive work, and verbally reward them if they have been serious in their effort. This will be a strengthening factor in developing the confidence necessary for sharing faith. By showing the work of all of your students you will be helping them to grow in their sense of personal value and worth as well as to meet other needs in the formation of a self-concept. Such other needs are, for example, providing the awareness of what they can do well and what they can't do well (be sensitive to whether they can accept this fact and help them to work it through if they can't), and what they understand and don't understand. Work closely with such students when assigning creative self-expression activities and help them to improve; don't spend all your time with the bright students.

The walls of the classroom, if light and clear, can be used for showing films or filmstrips or used with the overhead projector, thus eliminating the need for a projection screen. For further suggestions as to how to use the walls of the classroom, see the discussion regarding the bulletin board. Finally, a last caution: do not use cellophane tape, for it tends to remove the paint when pictures or displays are taken down, and, even if it does not remove the paint, often leaves marks. Masking tape is much better for attaching materials to the walls.

g. *Opaque Projector*

The opaque projector is an extremely helpful visual aid, for it can project any visual image from any source that can fit on the platform of the machine. Pictures, maps, graphs, or students' work can be projected for all to see while discussing the meaning of what is being viewed. The only drawbacks of this machine are its expense, weight (though newer ones are somewhat lighter in weight), and the fact that it can be used only in the dark.

h. *Overhead Projector*

The overhead projector provides what the opaque projector lacks, inexpensiveness and lighter weight; also, it can be used in a room that is not dark. However, the materials which are used with this machine have to be transparent. Hence you could not simply place a book on the machine and have it show a particularly valuable picture, as the opaque projector would be able to do. The picture would first have to be made into a transparency with the use of a copier (not all copiers are able to make transparencies from books). The 3-M Company has produced a series of religious transparencies for use by Protestant and Catholic churches, incorporating the relative theological differences into each respective set. Certain denominations and publishing houses are also beginning to produce overhead transparencies dealing with religious subjects. It is not necessary, however, that all that is shown on an overhead projector be printed material. Blank transparencies are available for writing and drawing, but require the use of special markers.

The advantages of using an overhead projector in your teaching are numerous: you can write while facing the class instead of turning your back as you must do when using the chalkboard; you can write the same way you would on paper instead of using the larger sweeping hand and arm movements necessary for writing on the chalkboard; the marks made by the special marking pencils are easily erased with a paper towel; and you have the interest feature that every machine has. The overhead is simple to operate, and it can project colors. It provides an unlimited space for writing, for when one transparency is filled, another can quickly be pressed into service, with the former one(s) brought back when you desire to review a point. Overheads now have an optional acetate roll which, when one section is all filled up, can be advanced for an immediate continuance of writing; the roll can be moved back easily for reviewing former material. It is also possible when using an overhead transparency to show only that part which you wish the students to see as you talk, advancing a blocking device to allow more of the transparency to be revealed as you proceed in your discussion. Opaque materials can be used to cast silhouettes on the screen. The use of silhouettes with this age group is limited, though one point which could be made after showing how different objects are all unique is that this is just the way we were all created and therein lies a positive value: we all, with our differences, have much to contribute.

As with the other visual aids, it helps when students are permitted to do the writing or drawing on the overhead. They will learn a lot by developing special overhead visuals for projection during the preparation of a project to which they have been assigned.

i. *Slide Transparencies*
The regular thirty-five millimeter slide transparencies which you take in your camera are also excellent re-

sources for teaching. Be constantly on the search for pictures that would provide helpful illustrations of certain concepts you will be teaching in the future as you vacation or take any trips. Often within your own locality you will find many subjects, a picture of which will provide a good visual illustration or point of discussion. Blank slides are also available on which you can print or draw your own illustrations for projection in a standard slide projector. Certain companies which publish church school curricula also produce transparencies that coincide with the subject matter.

j. Work Sheets

If your church has a spirit duplicator or a mimeograph machine, another visual aid that will prove helpful to you is the work sheet. Similar to a test but for use while studying a particular unit, the work sheet provides for the involvement of all the pupils in the learning process and is an effective tool for reinforcing what is being learned. Although a test provides the same qualities, the main purpose is what distinguishes the two teaching tools. A test is designed to determine how much the student has learned at the end of a particular unit of study, but a work sheet is used solely in class to promote pupil participation and reinforcement. The work sheet is not graded or marked by the teacher. It is simply a written exercise done in class in which the students answer the questions you have devised, then exchange papers and discuss the correct answers in class. The purpose of the work sheet is to give the student an opportunity to think through material he has recently been studying, and by means of this exercise to have another experience reinforcing what he has been learning and through which he can improve his ability to express himself and his faith.

k. *Individualized Programmed Instruction*

A final visual resource that is usable with junior high young people is individualized programmed instruction. This method is coming to receive much attention today, but as with many other teaching techniques that are being much talked about, it is one which has ancient roots. As it is being utilized today, however, it is the practice of arranging materials to be learned in a succession of small steps designed to help a student teach himself as he proceeds from the known to the unknown of new and more complex principles. Such instruction is being developed not only in visual but also in audio-visual form. In visual materials, there is the excellent study entitled *From Milk to Meat,* by Merle Farris, published in November of 1969, which is designed as a course for confirmation. This guide could be used in your situation as a textbook or, better, on an individual basis for students who finish their classwork early, or as an extraclass project in which you help each student individually. Although programmed instruction is designed for self-teaching, it is always so much better when a teacher is available for help when requested. Also, there is little to stop you from designing your own programming. All you need are some pointers regarding what special elements to include and exclude from your program, and an excellent book for such help is *A Guide to Programmed Instruction,* by Lysaught and Williams. This book is designed for secular education, but it is easily understood and transfer to your teaching situation will not be difficult. By studying the development of this technique, you will discover that you are becoming a better church school teacher as you grow in your ability to present material logically and in a meaningful sequence.

The results on your students will be even more impressive. In a study of the effect of programmed learning in the classroom, it was found that students involved in programming scored higher on standardized tests than did peers taught by conventional methods.[28] Programmed learning by itself is no panacea, but it offers great opportunities for the church school teacher.

3. *Audio-Visual Aids*

a. *Sixteen Millimeter Motion Picture*

In audio-visual combination, certainly one of the most familiar is the sixteen millimeter sound motion picture. Such films are becoming more accessible to the church school classroom because of their reasonable rental rates and the development of automatic-loading film projectors. In addition to the general cautions noted above pertaining to the use of audio-visual aids, care must be taken here to use whenever possible movies that are up to date. Showing a film in which the girls' hemlines are far below the knee (styles don't vary that quickly!) and the boys have short hair and thin coat lapels will not only cause distraction as comments are engendered among the style-conscious teens, but you will also be communicating a good deal concerning how relevant the church and God are to the life situation of your teens. It would be far better to omit an out-of-date film, even though it means altering your lesson plan, than to proceed because it is easier, for that would teach that Christian education and even God are irrelevant to the times and circumstances in which your young people exist.

b. *Sound Film Loop*

A recent development in film production has resulted in the creation of the sound film loop. Presently available on a limited basis in the religious field, it will be the film medium of the future for the classroom. Coming in eight millimeter cassettes, the sound film loop provides ease and flexibility for the viewing of films in the class context.

c. *Silent Film Loop*

Offering a wider range of subjects in the Christian faith is the silent film loop, an eight millimeter cassette device with a script that is read during the showing of the film by the teacher or a student. This medium of instruction as well as the sound film loop may be used in the same way as the conventional sixteen millimeter film.

d. *Filmstrips*

Today many excellent filmstrips are being produced at a very reasonable cost for purchase or rental. In fact, the price of purchase is so inexpensive that it is better if the church can purchase the filmstrip, for after as few as two or three showings, the strip would be paid for in equivalent rental fees. If your church has no such policy, try to encourage the people responsible to act accordingly.

Most filmstrips today are thirty-five millimeter and are coming out in full color with a recorded script. They appear in a wide range of subjects dealing with various dimensions of the Christian faith. They lend themselves especially to group discussion, for the strips can be stopped conveniently at any frame on which the teacher would like to focus the attention of the class for a particular analysis. This stop action can be effected on many sixteen millimeter projectors as well, but the picture is generally sharper and teachers usually feel more comfortable stopping the less complicated filmstrip machine. Most filmstrips average from ten to twenty minutes in running time and can be most any length, but there are a number of very small filmstrips called filmclips which average only eight to ten frames and are only a couple of minutes long. These filmclips are, however, very good for church school instruction, for the purpose of using such a visual aid is not to take up time but to provide an opportunity for the student to further reinforce what he is learning.

A relatively new adaptation of the thirty-five millimeter filmstrip is now being produced as a split/thirty-five millimeter filmstrip. Used best with an adapter for a regular thirty-five millimeter projector, these visual aids, one half the width of the thirty-fives, are excellent in the quality of the artwork they contain. Produced under the trade name Stori-Strip, they should be carefully selected for suitability for junior high young people. They cover a wide variety of subjects from Bible stories and an examination of the Near Eastern culture at the time of Jesus to a set relating science to the Christian faith. The latter two are especially good for junior high students and are the only sets available in the split/thirty-five series with recorded scripts designed especially for junior highs. These strips may be used in the same way other filmstrips are.

Currently on the market is an audio-visual aid that utilizes the filmstrip method and is called a phono-viewer, put out under the trade name Show 'N Tell. This is an excellent teaching machine for preschool, primary, and junior students, but this writer would not recommend its use with youth in the grade levels of six and above. It is unwise to use with youth a medium designed for children. Such use simply communicates that the gospel is not relevant for the junior high.

e. *Individualized Programmed Instruction*

In the near future an individualized programmed instruction machine based on the phono-viewer model will appear on the market; it is now in the first stage of mass production. A programmed audio-visual presentation of a life situation will appear on the screen, and after a brief time it will be stopped partway through and a question with four alternative answers will be shown. If the student pushes the wrong button on a panel before him corresponding to one of the four alternatives on the screen, his wrong answer will be recorded and a light will indicate his error. When he selects the right response, the program will continue with the next question. The device aids the student in analyzing the key elements in a situation and helps him to respond accordingly, thus applying the Christian faith to life situations. When it becomes available, this instructional aid can be used in the same manner as the visual programmed material discussed above, but it should produce even greater results in the areas in which the two overlap.

f. *Television*

Another teaching machine of the future for Christian education is television. While its greatest use in the local church will be in the years ahead, you can use it now in certain circumstances. Many good programs are being produced that are either religious in nature or which, though secular in content, have definite religious implications. Be looking for such programs coming up and when one is scheduled that relates directly to something you are studying, tell your class to be sure to watch it, and then discuss it at your next meeting. An even better approach is to invite your whole class over to your house to watch the show over potato chips and pop, and then have your first discussion concerning how what was seen related to what they are studying.

g. *Video Tape*

Lastly, an audio-visual aid that is very versatile, though as yet not within financial reach of the local Christian education program in most cases, is the video tape. However, the cost of such devices is becoming lower, and already some of the larger churches can afford them. Where this is not possible, you might encourage other churches to join with yours in a co-op which would buy and share not only this but other technological instructional machines. The uses of the video tape are all but unlimited, and in the future as they are modified even further, uses will increase. Certainly, the video tape can do everything the regular tape recorder can do, with the added plus of the visual dimension. Other uses of video tape include the later showing of good religious or secular TV programs that are televised when our youth cannot see them, the replay of films, the production of your own program, the recording of guest speakers for future use, and the preservation of special occasions. If you have the essential attribute of the Christian church school teacher, a desire to grow, you can tape classes and learn how you might have done certain things better as you watch the replay after a particular session.

These, then, are audio and visual aids that have usefulness to the learning situations of junior high youth. They should always be used with another method of learning, a type of group discussion, for example, in order best to reach the specific objective you have for their use. Yet there is another group of resources that can be used with audio-visuals, or as methods of communication in themselves. These will provide the main focus of our attention in the next chapter.

10
Creative Self-Expression Aids

SINCE WE ARE TRYING to minister to the junior high's needs, which include the psychological requirements to grow in intellectual ability and to incorporate all dimensions of his life into a meaningful identity, we will do well to provide opportunities in the church school context wherein the adolescent can achieve these ends. There are a number of resources that you can utilize in helping your young people meet these needs, participation in which will enable them to express themselves creatively and thereby to grow in their self-concept through discovering not only what they are able to do and do well but also what they believe. Furthermore, they will also grow in their ability to express their faith.

1. *Writing*

One of these resources is writing. As the junior high is capable of dealing in abstract formulation, it is good to have him write a composition from time to time on his understanding of a concept you have been just studying. For instance, you could ask each student to write a composition of at least one page on the subject "Redemption and What This Means to Me Personally" or "Sin and How

I Will Communicate This Concept." As the pupil is involved in the process of composing his paper, he will also be reinforcing what he is learning while he is developing the ability to communicate it.

2. Individual Drawing

Various forms of artwork also provide excellent media for learning. One such form is drawing, of which there are two kinds that can be used effectively with junior highs. You can assign individual drawing, where the student can create freehand impressions of his view of certain concepts and how they relate to him as a person, how they are incorporated into his personality. You could assign such a task as "Draw your concept of salvation." Care must be taken, however, to make such individual drawing freehand; otherwise, if you merely give students a picture to color they will react against it, rightly so, as beneath their level. Coloring books or pictures are designed for younger children who cannot express themselves abstractly. With your teens, however, free drawing with crayons, colored chalk, charcoal, or oil pastels will help them visualize the concept and further develop their understanding of it and how to express it.

3. Mural Drawing

Mural drawing is also a helpful tool. This art form can be used with small groups, where each subgroup of the class does a portion of the mural. A theme is decided upon—for instance, the events of Holy Week. Subgroups are formed and either assigned or allowed to choose an event of Holy Week which they want to portray on a mural. Then, meeting in subgroups, plans are made for laying out each section of the mural and someone chosen to draw each part. One subgroup will make a scene of

"The Triumphal Entry" and another, a scene of "The Last Supper." Then, within each subgroup, one student will draw the people waving palm branches while another draws the ass, and another, Jesus. When the mural has been completed, be sure to display it somewhere in the church building to give added significance to the activity. If your church has a church newspaper, have a couple of volunteers write a story about what the class did and why, and if pictures can be printed in your church newspaper, submit one of the mural with the story. Perhaps you could even hold it up and explain it during a worship service.

4. *Painting*

Another art form that produces the same results as drawing is painting. Do not shy away from such an activity because it could become a little messy. The rewards in terms of growth in your students are too great to be compromised for such a small inconvenience as making sure that each student is equipped with one of Dad's old white shirts as a smock. Painting can be used in the same manner as drawing.

5. *Motion Picture Film*

Students can make their own films as they write and draw on sixteen millimeter clear film leader. Such a medium provides for unlimited creativity, though it requires some effort to learn to reproduce enough parts of the images being shown in enough successive stages of development for the human eye to visualize and comprehend. However, this process is not as complicated as it may at first sound, and it is well within the capacity of your junior highs to perform. Also, a film- and slide-making kit, complete with all necessary materials and an instruction manual is available from the Griggs Educational Service, Livermore, California. The sound dimension of the presentation could readily be supplied with a tape recorder. In addition to interesting learning reinforcement, this method of teaching enables the student to sense accomplishment in a very vivid way as well as to gain insight into the logical sequence of events in the concept which he is developing.

6. *Clay, Papier-Mâché, and Plaster of Paris*

These substances provide excellent materials for the creation of three-dimensional art forms. An individual or group could be given the task of making a relief map of Palestine. Such a visual aid will be invaluable in clarifying much of their thinking concerning different Biblical accounts. For example, it will help them to see the element of sacrifice in the concept of service as they discover the nature of the Jericho road which falls so sharply and is so rough that it provides a place for bandits to hide and do harm. This element of service will add to the meaning of Jesus' parable of the good Samaritan, which is often missed when simply hearing it without seeing it in its context. They will discover that it was not an easy thing for the Samaritan to pack the injured man on his donkey and lead both down the rough road. The understanding that service can be difficult will help you effect transfer to their own situations. This understanding of the fact that service can be difficult is more readily acceptable to the adolescent than the incomplete concept that is often presented wherein the element of hardship on the part of the servant is missing. The student knows that it isn't easy to serve if he is really going to do it right, and if he is presented with only part of the picture, he will reject the concept as unrealistic. However, if he has been prepared with the proper understanding, he will be better able and more willing to cope with the reality when he encounters it.

7. *Snow Sculpturing*

In the wintertime you have all the materials available, if you live in the north, for snow sculpturing. The youngsters will enjoy creating concepts in the snow. This could be done in two operations, and the specific tasks could be planned in the same way as the mural work. For example, if you are studying the concept of grace, you could have one subgroup of the class create a display of Moses leading the Israelites out of Egypt. A head snowman could be leading a number of other snowmen between two huge mounds of snow (the waters of the Red Sea). A short distance away could be a snow sculpture of the incarnation, Jesus in the manger, Mary and Joseph. A little farther to the right could be the sculpture of a junior high helping someone in response to the grace of God as portrayed in the two Biblical accounts to the left. Thus is portrayed a progression from left to right of the Christian understanding of God's grace and man's response. The different sculptures could be identified with posters if desired or left to speak just as they are. This method of learning and communication will help greatly to provide not only greater understanding and ability in expressing that understanding but also an exciting class experience, as the young people enjoy Christian fellowship together while working at their tasks. This fellowship will help to meet their social needs which we have already discussed.

8. *Photography*

Photography is a medium that should be utilized in the learning experience. Students could be encouraged to portray photographically a concept about which you have been learning, or a student who has a special interest in photography could be allowed to make it his particular project. One can think of any number of subjects which when photographed would depict different dimensions of the meaning of love. An additional teaching aid involving photography has been produced by Eastman Kodak entitled "Photo-Story Discovery Set," available in color and black and white. It furthers the development of creative self-expression, and, conceivably, the class could produce its own sets along similar lines, but dealing with different situations.

9. *Drama*

Do not overlook drama as a fine opportunity for creative self-expression. The ideal would be to let a group in your class write and produce its own play depicting a particular concept and its relevance to the life situations of the junior highs. Perhaps the whole class would want to work on it, those interested in writing to prepare the script and those wanting to work on props to prepare the staging, and those wishing to act working in that area. If the class couldn't or felt that it didn't want to develop its own dramatic presentation, it could use one that has already been written. Such ready-made plays can be obtained at the Contemporary Drama Service of Downers Grove, Illinois.

Each student in the class should have a part in its production. Let those who want to have speaking parts try out for the ones they want in front of the whole class which then votes to determine who is the best for which part. An even more equitable way to divide responsibilities is through a drawing. However, if this method is used, be sure everyone is willing to do what is expected. If, for example, a very shy girl wound up with the lead in the play, you and she could be in for some anxious moments. Those who do not want to speak or those who are left after all speaking parts have been taken can work in any of the other equally important (though not as publicly visible—and this may open up a whole unit of study on values) areas of staging, publicity, and costumes. Or when there are not enough roles to go around, those who want a speaking part could learn a certain character's lines as an alternate. In any case, much learning and ability to communicate will take place as each student is involved in creating the different aspects of the play to portray accurately his understanding of a concept and its relation to his life.

10. *Collage*

A popular art form that is receiving much use because it works so well is the collage. This form of artistic expression denotes by its name a clustering together of fragments used to communicate thoughts about a concept. These fragments can be anything, and three-dimensional objects add much interest and color.

Use collages in your teaching with buzz groups. Divide your class into groups of three, and make sure each group has a sufficient supply of miscellaneous materials with which to work. (At the session before you determine to use this method encourage the youth to bring their own materials, but have some on hand in case they forget.) Explain their task to them very carefully. They are to search through all the items and select those to be pasted onto a piece of 8½″ x 11″ paper or cardboard. The finished product will show their impression of the concept of, for example, the church. Inform them that they will have ten minutes to select their materials, followed by three minutes to arrange and paste them together, after which they will meet for ten minutes in group discussion.

In the group discussion phase of their work, let the student with the earliest birthday in each buzz group begin by holding up his collage before the other two members of his team. Each student comments upon what he thinks the collage-maker is saying through his work. Then the person who made the collage adds to the comments made by the other two members of his subgroup. The process is repeated for each subgroup member. In the experience of this writer, this exercise always adds greatly to the understanding of each person of the concept being studied. Also, each person's ability to verbalize his growing understanding helps to increase his effectiveness in communicating his faith at that point.

11. *Montage*

The same procedure may also be used with a montage, a sister of the collage. This art form is made by combining different words and pictures which often overlap into a composite. Newspapers and magazines provide good materials for such work, the former for the words and the latter for their colorful photographs.

12. *Banner*

Another current much-used art form is the banner. Made to express a concept, it can be composed of cloth on cloth, acrylic paint on cloth, woven patterns, or any other combination that the student would like to try. The method of using banner-making in class could follow that used with collages. Wooden dowels can be purchased inexpensively in a local hardware or lumber supply store for the purpose of hanging the banner.

13. *Poster*

Posters are also popular with young people, and of all the art forms mentioned in this chapter they are perhaps the easiest to make. Often as simple as putting a few powerful words from a famous quotation on a background of vivid color, such a medium of communication can be dynamic. With posters, you want to encourage your students to put a great deal of thought into saying what they want to say in as few words as they can. Let the visual element of the work do as much speaking as possible, unless, as in the example just mentioned, only a very few words stand out. If a poster is to be effective, it must be understood at a glance by people trying to keep up with the hectic pace of twentieth-century American life. In making posters, you can use the method described above for collages.

14. *Mobile*

The mobile art form may also be used successfully with junior highs. First the superstructure can be fashioned, using wire from coat hangers, and then three circles could be made for hanging on the mobile. In one circle hang symbols which the Old Testament used to describe God (rock, shield, horn), in the second circle, one or more symbols from the New Testament (a cross, a fire, a two-edged sword), and in the third circle, symbols which we use today in referring to God (perhaps a heart symbolizing love, an electric transformer to represent God as power, a man's head to symbolize God as mind or intelligence). This method can be used very well in three small groups, each group being responsible for one of the circles, and each member of the group contributing one of the symbols for their circle. This procedure would require Bible study and discussion in addition to group cooperation in the physical activity.

15. *Ceramics*

Ceramics also present excellent opportunities for communication. Working either as individuals or in groups, students can use this art form for communicating Biblical concepts in a very contemporary and realistic way. Any local art supplies retailer can guide you as to what materials you need and how to use them. If you cannot find such a place in the telephone directory, consult the art teacher at your area high school.

16. *Singing*

As a rule, junior high students today do not like singing in the church school. However, this appears to be true only when the students cannot select the songs they will sing. In conversations this writer has had with junior high young people from different parts of the country, it is clear that they like to sing when singing is meaningful (not, for example, as an automatic and mechanical means of opening a meeting) and when they can select the songs they will sing. They are not "turned on" by much of the old gospel tunes of the past three centuries which appear in the hymnbooks of most evangelical churches at the present time. They are, though, quite drawn to some new songs that have lyrics expressing Biblical theology in the thought forms of youth, with which they can identify, and which are set to the tune of music that is also expressive of youthful mentality. It is no wonder that they like to tune in to this type of music, for it is relevant to their own life situations.

It is important that you familiarize yourself with this music by talking with your teens and by writing to the department of youth work in your denomination. Get to know who in your class can play musical instruments, especially the guitar, the instrument most closely related to this type of music. Plan a singing unit in advance with some members of your class and decide ahead of time when it would be good to try to express in music some of the concepts you have been studying. Many contemporary songs add much insight and provide much transfer of learning for such concepts as love, forgiveness, church, and service. Singing also has an important function pertaining to worship within the education context. This usage will be considered further in the next chapter.

Older hymns do have a use. In a unit of study on church history, for instance, the singing of hymns from certain periods would be a fine method of helping the students to put themselves back into that time mentally as well as helping them to appreciate and capture some of the contributions made by those periods. It is good to teach the importance of the past, but be sure to make your strongest singing emphasis one that is most relevant to your students. Such activity will provide a psychological binding and group consciousness which will greatly aid in meeting their sociopsychological needs, as well as teach much concerning the nature of the church.

17. *Newspaper*

A final method for creative self-expression is that of making a youth newspaper, an excellent tool for Bible study. The class could put out an issue as an "extra" as if prepared on the day of the resurrection of Christ. Some members of the class could be reporters writing factual accounts of the story and recording man-on-the-street interviews; other students could write editorials on the event; others could send in letters to the editor expressing their opininon as to the significance of the resurrection. Those in your class who can draw could make pictures for the newspaper showing different aspects of the event including the open tomb, Jesus talking to Mary, Thomas feeling Jesus' wounds, and Jesus' response. The paper then could be mimeographed or processed on a spirit duplicator. Another use of the newspaper method would be to publish a regular issue periodically which would include news items of and by junior high young people dealing with all dimensions of their lives and containing feature articles on their understanding of different Biblical concepts, especially as they relate to the situations they encounter daily.

In the newspaper method of teaching as well as in the other methods, it is important to involve all the students in the project. Make sure that each is responsible for a certain area, so that he can have the experience of making a contribution. The newspaper will give each youth the opportunity to express what is *him* in his own way, further enabling him to grow in his own self-understanding and ability to communicate.

One other resource for presentation yet remains to be discussed, and that is worship. It is to this important subject that we now turn our attention.

11
Worship

WHY SHOULD THE CHAPTER ON WORSHIP appear almost at the end instead of at the beginning of a study on Christian education? The answer is basically that one does not start out worshiping God until he has learned about God. It is a matter of logical sequence.

We began with the assumption that we are using the whole Bible as the basic resource in class. Our students, therefore, have learned about God, and it is partly our responsibility and partly our privilege to encourage their desire to worship. How? There is nothing you can do to force worship (I Cor. 12:3), but you can and should provide the opportunity for it to take place, and you can encourage it by your own example, as we shall soon see.

In the Sunday school we have inherited a form of worship that in most cases with which this writer is familiar is proving less than satisfactory for junior highs. When the Sunday school system was first established and was rejected by the organized church, it had to have its own time of worship along with the learning experience so that the unchurched children whom it was trying to reach would have at least some opportunity to worship. However, as the Sunday school became accepted by the church down through the years, it and its system both came intact, even though a regular service of worship usually followed the Sunday school program of learning.

The main faults of such a vestigial worship experience in Sunday school are that it is mechanical and automatic (which would seem to be just what God doesn't want man's response to be, the reason why he gave man a free will), that it uses forms (the lecture type and the arrangement of students in rows) and means (hymnody from another generation) which are not expressions of worship with which the junior high can identify. In worship one extends *himself,* not a wooden and static formula, to God. Hence, what often happens is that instead of having available a resource for education, the teacher faces an obstacle that causes discipline problems. How, then, can the teacher effect a more meaningful experience in worship as the junior high's vertical response to his learning?

First of all, let worship arise out of a point in study where it is most meaningful and natural. For example, when completing a unit of study where a young person has discovered the meaning and purpose he has in life through Christ, you could be instrumental in leading your class to a moving experience in worship by saying something like, "You know, this insight that God uses my life so meaningfully makes me feel like worshiping him. How do you feel?" Where the students have been able to participate in the learning experience, they too will have a similar feeling and undoubtedly reply in the affirmative, which will result in a significant response in worship.

Such a response can take the form of group singing, using any of the number of excellent youth songs that express concepts meaningful to them. Another form that your students may wish to use is the sacred dance, in which several persons accompanied by music pantomime their feelings as they express themselves to God with their whole personality. The students may wish to use prayer as a form of worship. An especially significant way to communicate in prayer is to do so in groups of three where each person has the opportunity to pray personally about things that concern him and to ask God's help for the others and the needs they have expressed. If such is the case, you may be wondering what to do about prayer in the individual class sessions. When it is not done in a ho-hum, automatic way, it is good to open a session with prayer in order to open ourselves to God's help in achieving our objectives.

The fact that we first learn about God and what he has done for us before becoming motivated to worship him does not mean that we hold off worshiping until we have reached a certain point of supposed perfection: for example, until we no longer have any questions or until we have memorized a whole catechism. Such a stance is neither Biblical nor reasonable, for man who is finite and limited cannot comprehend God who is infinite and unlimited. There will never be a time in this phase of our lives when we will have *all* our questions answered, so we should not try to reach a certain academic level before drawing worship into the educational experience.

Also, as I Cor. 12:3 indicates, the Holy Spirit is active in the world. Hence, revelation is a very real learning experience, and we would be remiss in Christian education not to allow an opportunity for him to bring about learning and growth in our lives. Not to provide for a worship experience in which the Holy Spirit could work would be to cut ourselves off from a vital resource.

But this experience cannot be forced in an automatic

manner. It must be done at a time when the heart and mind become receptive to the working of the Spirit. Such was the practice of the ancient believer. When he became aware of God's grace, he responded in gratitude. Consider these passages from Ps. 107:

> O give thanks to the LORD, for he is good;
>   for his steadfast love endures for ever!
> Let the redeemed of the LORD say so.
>
> Some wandered in desert wastes, . . .
> hungry and thirsty. . . .
> Then . . . he delivered them from their distress.
> Let them thank the LORD for his steadfast love.
>
> Some sat in darkness and in gloom. . . .
> Then . . . he delivered them from their distress.
> Let them thank the LORD for his steadfast love.
>
> Some were sick. . . .
> Then . . . he sent forth his word, and healed them.
> Let them thank the LORD for his steadfast love.
>
>   (Ps. 107:1–21.)

The Biblical response to grace is gratitude. Man responds to God's grace by offering heartfelt thanks and honoring him. When through discussion of how God has been working in the lives of fellow class members a student sees himself in relation with that God, learning takes place and his response is to stand in awe and offer praise or, in a word, worship.

Thus worship is both a means of learning and a response to learning, but it is primarily the latter. One cannot start out worshiping an unknown entity, and once God is known, the learner must become motivated to worship him. Although in Christian education we spend much time in the important area of helping students to come to know

Christ and how he relates to them, we must also create the opportunity where they can deepen their relationship with the Lord, responding to his love with theirs, and allowing him further to nurture them according to his plan for their lives.

In these ways worship takes on a high value, and it becomes a resource in Christian education that is without equal in relating faith to life's needs. It is no longer a time-consuming activity; it has a valid and integral place in the Christian nurture of our young people.

We have now studied the needs of the junior high and have planned a class session that would utilize the best methods whereby those needs could be met. There is yet one task remaining before us: to determine whether or not we have met those needs once we have completed our unit of study. Such evaluation of our efforts is the subject to which we now turn our attention.

PART IV

EVALUATION

Evaluating Students and Teachers

1. *Evaluating the Student*

a. *Formal Evaluation*

After you have completed a unit of study, how can you determine whether you have attained your goals? To find out it is necessary to measure the amount of learning your students have acquired. How do you do this? The best way is to offer a written test including only those areas incorporated by your objectives. The objectives themselves may serve as some of the questions that appear on the examination.

However, since the junior high is intellectually capable of and has the need to think conceptually, and since it is important that he be able to make the transfer of what he learns in theory to how he will apply it in practice in his daily life, a proper test of his growth should include one or more subjective questions. In fact, since it is important at this age level to challenge and stimulate the student to use his intellectual ability to think propositionally, and since by this time he will in most cases have had much learning in the factual data of the Bible, your test should be more subjective than objective.

Obviously, one cannot develop concepts without precepts. And it is important to include some factual questions, albeit a small percentage of the total, in an evaluation. However, great care should be taken at this point, for it is quite difficult to develop objective questions that are fair and unambiguous, especially for the junior high, who is beginning to be able to think conceptually and sees that the answers to all questions are not simply black or white. When composing factual questions, select only those most basic to the student's desired level of attainment and be very sure that they are not obscure in any way, that is, be certain that *under no circumstances* could another answer besides the one you want be valid. For example, do not have a question like this: "Jesus Christ brings peace for all people who accept him. True or False _____." The junior high who is thinking will likely recall John 14:27 on the one hand, and Matt. 10:34 on the other. Hence, from a Scriptural point of view this true or false question is both true and false depending upon how it is taken in context. But there is no context given; it is only an objective statement, and it is ambiguous. The student taking the test does not know how you are using the sentence. As it stands, either answer is permissible from a Biblical perspective, so you cannot mark either wrong, and you cannot ascertain an evaluation.

When using objective questions, therefore, be sure to make them concrete, for example, "Moses led the people of Israel across the Nile. True or False _____." Another suggestion, especially for true or false questions, is to have the student cross out the wrong part of the question and write in the correct response. Hence, in the above question "Nile" would be marked out and "Red Sea" would be written above. Such a practice also helps to control guessing.

In structuring subjective questions, try to couch the query in terms dealing with the life situations being encountered by adolescents. For example: "You are in another city visiting a friend. One of the subjects you discuss while talking with your friend is the relationship between God and man. Your friend says to you, 'Well, look at all the good man does today: doctors take care of the sick; there are so many charities which give to the poor; all of our neighbors are the nicest people you could meet—I don't think that man is sinful by nature.' From what you have learned, what would you say to your friend?"

Such questions may be a little more difficult to form, especially at first, and to correct, but they will be much more meaningful for each student, for they will help him to relate what he is learning to situations he meets in life. How much learning you help your student achieve will be determined by whether you put forth just that little extra effort which may make a huge difference in how real his faith is. Quite soon you will develop the ability to structure subjective questions in a minimum of time with a maximum of quality.

Do not grade the tests, for this introduces a competitive element which, as we have seen, is not desirable. We are interested only in having a student compete with himself and not with others. Hence, correct the tests, writing in the margin your comments, and hand them back to the students to go over in class, discussing the answers.

As a motivating factor for the students to do serious work, tell them that tests will be held frequently (give fair notice always ahead of time when you are planning an evaluation), as often as once a month, and that at different times during the year at test will be sent home to Mom and Dad, no one knowing which of his tests will be the one that is sent home. Then be sure to do what you say—a cardinal rule in education—always follow through on your promise. This statement puts the exercise in an even more meaningful light; it is not thought of as busy-work. In the minds of the students the test becomes a serious business, and hence a valuable learning experience.

b. *Informal Evaluation*

Up to this point, we have been considering the formal evaluation of a student's work. Before we consider the evaluation of the teacher, a comment concerning the informal evaluation of a pupil's learning is necessary.

Evaluation is not only a once-a-month or occasional practice. The good teacher is always evaluating both his own and his students' work. Evaluation is an ongoing process, and informal, on-the-spot evaluation is very important. For example, if your students in preparing a play expressing their understanding of a concept and its relation to their lives begin to express a thought that is unbiblical, you have a perfect teaching opportunity to help them work through their thinking to a more Scriptural response. They can evaluate their thought and exercise their power of reversibility by backing up to where their logic departed from the norm and, with your help, rethink their stand. Here is another way the pupil participation principle greatly aids learning; such a situation might not occur were it not for the free flow of ideas and hence an errant thought might not be discovered.

2. *Evaluating the Teacher*

In evaluating yourself, you must have incorporated into your self-concept the Biblical realization of human fallibility: you can and you will err. So *desire* evaluation in order to find out how you can improve. You are not a fount of all knowledge. Unlike God, you are not omniscient. You need help to find out how to do better, so where do you look?

a. *Examine the students' tests.*

The first place to look is at the results of the students' tests. The test the student takes not only tells the student and you as the teacher where the student needs more help, how much he has retained, what subjects ought to be covered again, and how well transfer has been effected, but it also tells you whether you are proceeding too slowly or too rapidly or just about right. It reveals whether anything and what has been communicated to your class. It shows you whether you have motivated your students to learn. And all these insights are frightening. However, if you have a realistic self-concept, your ego will be able to withstand the blow. Be comforted with the assurance that the best teacher in the world can still grow; both he and his students are human.

b. *Establish a climate of openness to sharing observations.*

It is well to establish a climate in your class wherein your students can feel comfortable in coming to you with suggestions for improvement. Such a feeling will help your relationship with your youth, for they will be able to identify with you, and you will thus be helping them to build a sound self-concept for themselves. This strong relationship will help to provide a healthy atmosphere in which mutual growth can take place for students and teacher alike, so both can benefit from each other's suggestions.

c. *Ask other teachers.*

A helpful form of evaluation for you to utilize is the objective observation of another teacher, the department chairman or the church school superintendent. The key to the effectiveness of such help, however, lies with you. You must sincerely desire honest opinions from the students, teachers, chairmen, and superintendents you ask. Do not tell them that you want their frank observations and then resent them when they are given.

d. *Make regular consultation of a guideline.*

Develop a list of key questions that will provide a guideline for the betterment of your teaching. Include in the list questions such as: (1) What percentage of all the talking that is done in the class do I do? (If it is over 50 percent, watch out!) (2) Is my preparation thorough or hastily put together the day before class? (3) Do I *love* each of my students as my own son or daughter in Christ? (4) Do I become impatient quickly? (5) What teacher-training meetings have I attended this year? (6) What books have I read lately that will help me teach better? (7) What teaching aids have I used during this past month? (Compare with the complete list available for your use.) (8) Whom have I asked to help me evaluate my teaching objectively? (9) Do I read the Bible regularly? (10) Do I pray constantly for help from God? (11) Do I pray regularly for my students and encourage them to pray for each other and me? (12) Do I provide a model in my own life of what I believe and teach? (13) Is what I do pointing to God or to me?

Be encouraged knowing that:

> All the ways of a man are pure in his own eyes,
>   but the LORD weighs the spirit.
> Commit your work to the LORD,
>   and your plans will be established.
>
>   (Prov. 16:2–3.)

APPENDIX A
Sample Lesson Plan Guide

LESSON PREPARATION—*Sheet No. 1*

THE NEEDS OF MY STUDENTS

NOTE: There is no area below entitled "Spiritual Needs." This is so because, Biblically speaking, a human being does not have a spiritual segment of his life separable from the other aspects of his total person. Rather, his whole self, everything that he is, exists in relation to God. Hence, his physical, social, and psychological needs will all have importance to you, for they all have theological implications. These three aspects of a person's life are all dealt with in the context of his relationship to God. Christ is Lord over all of a person's life, not just a part (a fourth) of it, and Christ's message speaks to all his needs, not to just one or two. In the teaching ministry we attempt to meet all of a person's needs through Christ our Lord.

I. Physical Needs

II. Social Needs

III. Psychological Needs

LESSON PREPARATION—*Sheet No. 2*

ORGANIZATION AND PRESENTATION

I. Organization (for the purpose of establishing *objectives*).
NOTE: Goals (broad, general aims) are attained through a comparison of the unit to be taught with Sheet No. 1, "The Needs of My Students."
   A. The Lesson Subject Matter
      1. Title
      2. Relationship to unit (how it fits into the theme of the unit)
   B. The Scripture Passage
      1. Historical background
         a. Who is writing the passage?
         b. To whom is he writing?
         c. Why is he writing (what is the situation causing him to write)?
         d. What essentially (in your own words) is he saying?
      2. Key words and phrases in the passage
         a. To discuss for understanding
         b. To use in forming objectives
      3. Message to pupils and to me in the twentieth century

II. The Method of Presentation
   A. The Tools I Will Use
      1. Methods for communication
      2. Illustrations
      3. Audio-visuals
      4. Mimeographed or other copied material to hand out
      5. Other tools
   B. The Tools Each Pupil Will Use
      1. Textbook(s)
      2. Other tools

APPENDIX B
Sample Written Exercise

THREE-MINUTE TIME TEST
Can You Follow Directions ? ? ? ? ? ?

1. Read everything before doing anything.
2. Put your name in the upper right-hand corner of this page.
3. Circle the word "name" in sentence 2.
4. Draw five small squares in the upper left-hand corner of this page.
5. Put an *X* in each square.
6. Put a circle around each square.
7. Sign your name under the title of this paper.
8. After the title write: Yes, Yes, Yes.
9. Put a circle around sentence 7.
10. Place an *X* in the lower left-hand corner of the page.
11. Draw a triangle around the *X* you have just made.
12. On the back of this paper multiply: 703 by 66.
13. Draw a circle around the word "paper" in sentence 7.
14. Loudly call out your first name when you get to this point.
15. If you have followed directions carefully to this point, call out, "I have."
16. On the reverse side of this paper add: 8,950 and 9,805.
17. Put a circle around your name, then put a square around the circle.
18. Count out in a normal speaking voice from one to ten *backward.*

19. Punch three small holes in the top of this paper with your pencil point.

20. If you are the first person to get this far, call out in a loud voice, "I am the leader in following directions."

21. Underline all even numbers on this side of the page.

22. Call out loudly, "I am nearly finished, and I have followed directions."

23. Now that you have finished reading carefully, do only sentences 1 and 2.

(Author Unknown.)

The "Three-Minute Time Test" has a number of possible uses with different units of study. One use is that it can teach a great deal about the nature and effects of sin. This exercise helps us discover that we, like Adam and Eve, do not follow directions—since very few of your students who have never seen this game before will read it all the way through as instructed—we disobey because of our own pride which makes us fear being last and drives us to be first in spite of what we should do.

In making the application, be sure to point out that we did not even get past the very first direction without disobeying. Show how we proved this by verbalizing our misdeeds with the words in sentences 15, 20, and 22. The conclusion will leave no doubt as the learner painfully discovers the truth you are trying to teach with this exercise.

APPENDIX C
Discipline

Aside from occasional comments indicating that certain techniques or activities would help relieve discipline problems, we did not deal with the subject of discipline per se in our study. The reasons for such an omission are twofold: (1) the Bible clearly places the practice of discipline in the hands of parents (e.g., Prov. 13:24; 19:18; 22:6; 29:15–17; Eph. 6:4), and (2) by following the suggestions discussed above, you will find as the author has found that your discipline problems will be minimal if not nonexistent.

However, since parents are not entirely keeping up their responsibility, it is necessary to make some suggestions which can serve as guidelines for dealing with discipline cases. We can identify at least five:

1. *Love your students.*

In approaching a class for the first time (and each class has a potential discipline problem), begin with prevention. In other words, you are going to be mainly instrumental in setting the atmosphere of the class. Your love and acceptance of the youngsters will be contagious, and, moreover, it will be teaching an important Scriptural truth about our relationship to God, for "we love, because he first loved us" (I John 4:19) and "while we were yet sinners Christ died for us" (Rom. 5:8).

Recognize the conflicts your teens are encountering in their physical, social, and psychological development, and you will be better able to understand and accept certain actions as a result of these forces. Remember how you feel and act when things don't go well for you on certain days.

2. *Consider whether you are meeting your students' needs.*
Evaluate frequently whether you are meeting the needs of your students. What have you been doing in class to meet their physical, social, and psychological growth requirements? Have you involved them in participatory learning methods which provide not only a channel for their energies but also an opportunity for them to discover concepts, retain them, and transfer them to their life situations? How?

3. *Don't be disturbed by noise.*
Approach your class with the attitude that all noise is not bad. In fact, when it is constructive, noise is very much to be desired. You can tell whether it is constructive if it is coming from students who are actively involved in working out a task that has been designed to meet one of your objectives. For instance, the humming of buzz groups disturbs no one even at close hand, but produces great results when it occurs in accomplishing a specific end.

4. *Know your students personally.*
Become close friends with your students—not in the sense of becoming one of them and losing your identity—but in the sense that you become a confidant and counselor. Meet your pupils individually and get to know their special struggles, especially difficulties that would be apparent in class, such as a weak self-concept, a sense of inferiority that would make them want to receive much attention, conceived of as recognition of importance.

5. *Develop a threefold plan for order.*
Finally, when you see that you still have a discipline problem on your hands, announce to your class that you follow a threefold plan regarding class order: "(*a*) I give one warning to stop disruptive behavior; (*b*) if the misbehavior occurs again after the warning, the person causing the trouble leaves the classroom, and (*c*) if the same student causes the same trouble the next week, he leaves the class for good until his parents (one or both) bring him back." In using this method, be sure to give *only one* warning and *stick to it!* If you keep

giving warnings and never get to the second step, your students will never take you seriously, but they will "take you for a ride." If you find it necessary to dismiss a student from the classroom, send only one, not the others with whom he was in communication, or else you will have pandemonium in the hall to your own frustration and embarrassment. In using both steps (a) and (b), be firm but loving, not judgmental or intolerant. In discipline, love and firmness go together; either without the other is not discipline.

If you follow the first two steps, you may find that you do not need to resort to the third step, one which very, very few students want to see happen. And if it is done only once, you will likely have little trouble from then on. You not only are perfectly proper in involving the parents with what is their God-given province, but it has been found that when this happens most children will alter their aberrant behavior.

Notes

1. *The Grand Rapids Press,* Dec. 12, 1969, p. 12-B.
2. *Ibid.*
3. An excellent graded sex education curriculum has been published by the Concordia Publishing House, St. Louis, Missouri. See also the book by Charlie W. Shedd in "Selected Readings."
4. Margaret Mead, *Coming of Age in Samoa* (The New American Library of World Literature, Inc., 1949), p. 13.
5. Erik H. Erikson, *Childhood and Society,* 2d rev. ed. (W. W. Norton & Company, Inc., 1963), p. 36.
6. Arthur T. Jersild, *The Psychology of Adolescence* (The Macmillan Company, 1957), p. 80.
7. Bayard Hooper, "The Real Change Has Just Begun," *Life,* Jan. 9, 1970, p. 105.
8. Dan Golenpaul (ed.), *Information Please Almanac, Atlas and Yearbook 1970* (Dan Golenpaul Associates, 1969), p. 633.
9. Bärbel Inhelder and Jean Piaget, *The Growth of Logical Thinking from Childhood to Adolescence,* tr. by Anne Parsons and Stanley Milgram (London: Routledge & Kegan Paul, Ltd., 1958), p. 336.
10. *Ibid.,* p. 1.
11. Ronald Goldman, *Religious Thinking from Childhood to Adolescence* (London: Routledge & Kegan Paul, Ltd., 1964), pp. 54, 58.
12. Matthew Arnold, "Dover Beach," in Bernard D. N. Grebanier, *et al.* (eds.), *From the Forerunners of Romanti-*

cism to the Present, Vol. II of *English Literature and Its Backgrounds,* rev. ed. (The Dryden Press, Inc., 1949), p. 588.

13. Socony-Vacuum Oil Company, study distributed through the Division of Church Life and Mission, Reformed Church in America, 475 Riverside Drive, New York, N.Y.

14. Division of Church Life and Mission, Reformed Church in America.

15. Herbert J. Klausmeier, *Learning and Human Abilities: Educational Psychology* (Harper & Brothers, 1961), p. 184.

16. *Ibid.,* p. 189.

17. Jerome P. Lysaught and Clarence M. Williams, *A Guide to Programmed Instruction* (John Wiley & Sons, Inc., 1963), p. 7.

18. Ted Ward, "Youth—The Vocal Majority," an address at the Christian Education Leadership Seminar "Implications for Church Education in the '70s," Cincinnati, Oct. 22, 1969. Dr. Ward is Director of the Learning Systems Institute and Human Learning Research Institute, Michigan State University.

19. Goldman, *op. cit.,* pp. 80–84.

20. Klausmeier, *op. cit.,* p. 344.

21. *Ibid.*

22. Goldman, *op. cit.,* p. 31.

23. John Calvin, *Institutes of the Christian Religion,* 2 vols. (The Library of Christian Classics), ed. by John T. McNeill, tr. by Ford Lewis Battles (The Westminster Press, 1960), III. ii. 7, p. 551.

24. *The Heidelberg Catechism,* tr. by Allen O. Miller and M. Eugene Osterhaven (The Reformed Church in America, 1962), p. 27.

25. J. D. Salinger, *The Catcher in the Rye* (Signet Book, The New American Library of World Literature, Inc., 1945), p. 156.

26. Paul H. Vieth, "Audio-Visual Method and Content," *Orientation in Religious Education,* ed. by Philip Henry Lotz (Abingdon-Cokesbury Press, 1950), p. 150.

27. *Ibid.,* p. 152.

28. Lysaught and Williams, *op. cit.,* p. 155.

Selected Readings

Articles

McCaffrey, Patrick J., "The Film and Religious Education," *Ave Maria* magazine, Nov. 11, 1967.

Pohlman, Edward W., "Infant Experience and Human Beliefs About Ultimate Causes," *The Journal of Pastoral Care,* Spring, 1965.

Porter, Donald W., "Let's Quit Playing Sunday School," *Christian Herald,* Feb., 1970.

Whitbread, Jane, "The Myth of the Normal Child," *Redbook,* Oct., 1968.

Books

Bauer, W. W. (ed.), *Today's Health Guide.* American Medical Association, 1965.

Bowman, Locke E., Jr., *Straight Talk About Teaching in Today's Church.* The Westminster Press, 1967.

Dollard, John; Doob, Leonard W.; Miller, Neal E.; Mowrer, O. H.; Sears, Robert R., *et al., Frustration and Aggression.* Yale University Press, 1939.

Douglass, Paul F., *The Group Workshop Way in the Church.* Association Press, 1956.

Erikson, Erik H., *Childhood and Society,* 2d rev. ed. W. W. Norton & Company, Inc., 1963.

Gesell, Arnold; Ilg, Frances L.; and Ames, Louise R., *Youth: The Years from Ten to Sixteen.* Harper & Brothers, 1956.

Ginott, Haim G., *Between Parent and Teenager*. The Macmillan Company, 1969.

Goldman, Ronald, *Readiness for Religion: A Basis for Developmental Religious Education*. London: Routledge & Kegan Paul, Ltd., 1965.

———— *Religious Thinking from Childhood to Adolescence*. London: Routledge & Kegan Paul, Ltd., 1964.

Howe, Reuel L., *The Miracle of Dialogue*. The Seabury Press, 1963.

Inhelder, Bärbel, and Piaget, Jean, *The Growth of Logical Thinking from Childhood to Adolescence,* tr. by Anne Parsons and Stanley Milgram. London: Routledge & Kegan Paul, Ltd., 1958.

Jersild, Arthur T., *Child Psychology*. Prentice-Hall, Inc., 1960.

———— *The Psychology of Adolescence*. The Macmillan Company, 1957.

Klausmeier, Herbert J., *Learning and Human Abilities: Educational Psychology*. Harper & Brothers, 1961.

Krech, David, and Crutchfield, Richard S., *Elements of Psychology*. Alfred A. Knopf, Inc., 1958.

LeBar, Lois E., *Focus on People in Church Education*. Fleming H. Revell Company, 1968.

Leypoldt, Martha M., *Forty Ways to Teach in Groups*. Judson Press, 1967.

Lysaught, Jerome P., and Williams, Clarence M., *A Guide to Programmed Instruction*. John Wiley & Sons, Inc., 1963.

Mager, Robert F., *Developing Attitude Toward Learning*. Fearon Publishers, Inc., 1968.

———— *Preparing Instructional Objectives*. Fearon Publishers, Inc., 1962.

Missildine, W. Hugh, *Your Inner Child of the Past*. Simon and Schuster, Inc., 1963.

Shedd, Charlie W., *The Stork Is Dead*. Word Books, 1968.

Smith, Barbara, *How to Teach Junior Highs*. The Westminster Press, 1965.

Thelen, Herbert A., *Dynamics of Groups at Work*. The University of Chicago Press, 1954.

Van Dyke, Vonda Kay, *Dear Vonda Kay*. Fleming H. Revell Company, 1967.

Vieth, Paul H., "Audio-Visual Method and Content," *Orientation in Religious Education,* ed. by Philip Henry Lotz. Abingdon-Cokesbury Press, 1950.
———— *How to Teach in the Church School.* Board of Christian Education, Presbyterian Church U.S.A., 1935.
Wattenberg, William W., *The Adolescent Years.* Harcourt, Brace & Co., Inc., 1955.

Index

Activating the God-given potential of the most mystifying age group—early adolescents

Teaching Early Adolescents Creatively

A MANUAL FOR CHURCH SCHOOL TEACHERS

by Edward D. Seely

"The early adolescent is beginning to forge a self-concept out of a cauldron of changes." Communicating the message of the Christian faith to young people of the junior high or middle school age group demands all the creativity that a teacher can muster.

This book is especially helpful to beginning teachers, giving insight into the pupils' physical and social concerns, their intellectual and emotional development. It helps teachers set realistic goals so they can go beyond simply "meeting the needs" of students. Uncommon resources, fresh methods of teaching, unusual learning experiences—all are combined in one package to give confidence and direction to any teacher.

EDWARD D. SEELY is Minister of Education at the Fifth Reformed Church, Grand Rapids, Michigan. A graduate of Hope College and Western Theological Seminary, he is also Junior High Youth Consultant for the Synod of Michigan.

THE WESTMINSTER PRESS

ISBN 0-664-24927-2

0778